How to
Read a
Church
Pocket
Guide

How to Read a Church
Pocket Guide

Richard Taylor

✣

Page 1 *The cross depicting Christ and St Cedd at the church of St Peter-on-the-Wall, Bradwell-on-Sea, Essex. Constructed in 650 using stone from an old Roman fort, and restored in 1920, this is the oldest church building in England.*

Page 2 *'Not my will but thine be done.' (Luke 22:42): Jesus, with cruciform halo, prays to God the Father, during the Agony in the Garden (p.171).*

Page 3 *Stained-glass window chalice in form of tree*

Opposite *A modern take on the Nativity, in a stained-glass window in the Netherlands. The growing tree in the background may represent new life for the world, given through the birth of Jesus. Joseph's caring expression emphasises his devotion and kindness.*

Overleaf *A row of angels in Augustus Pugin's Neo-Gothic masterpiece the church of St Giles, Cheadle, Staffordshire. Almost every surface is brightly coloured with tiles, paint or gilding.*

1 3 5 7 9 10 8 6 4 2

Published in 2007 by Rider, an imprint of Ebury Publishing

A Random House Group Company

Addresses for companies within the Random House Group can be found at
www.randomhouse.co.uk

A CIP catalogue record for this book is available from the British Library

The Random House Group Limited makes every effort to ensure that the
papers used in our books are made from trees that have been legally sourced
from well-managed and credibly certified forests. Our paper procurement
policy can be found on www.randomhouse.co.uk

To buy books by your favourite authors and register for offers visit
www.rbooks.co.uk

Edited by Pamela Todd
Designed by David Fordham

Printed and bound in Singapore by Tien Wah Press

ISBN 9781846040733

Manus Dei *emerging from clouds, carved on exterior of the church
of St Michael, Garway, Herefordshire, a church originally built by
the Knights Templar in the 1180s.* Overleaf, *The Saxon church
of St Mary, Breamore, Hampshire, which dates from c. 980.*

CONTENTS

AUTHOR'S NOTE

TRINITY—EACH DIVINE PERSON WEARING THE CRU

The ability to read a church – to interpret the images, signs, and symbols – is a skill now rare, even among regular churchgoers. At the same time, these sites remain focal points in communities, and visiting them is as popular as ever. The purpose of this book is to help visitors to churches, whether occasional sightseers or regular attenders, and of any faith or none, to understand the richness and depth of what they find around them. You will by no means see every image described in this book when you visit a church, and you may find many that are not. As fashions have changed over the centuries, churches have been built with varying degrees of decoration. Some are very plain, while others are highly ornate and the representations in them may extend to less common examples. Some emphasize local saints, or the particular spiritual or political concerns of the patron or builders. This book is an overview and explanation of the most common images.

Language can be a troublesome medium, which symbols and images can be useful in transcending. To steer clear of this kind of trouble, I need to explain some of the language that I will be using.

✣

The altar frontal (above) *at the church of St James the Great, Audlem, Cheshire. The design shows a cross bearing the letters 'IHS' and images of grapes, vine leaves and wheat.*

Church / church

Early Christians did not meet in buildings dedicated to worship, but in common meeting places or one another's homes. The word 'church', therefore, referred to a body of Christian believers. Nowadays the word retains this meaning, as well as referring to the building that Christians worship in. To distinguish them, when referring to a body of Christians, I use a capital 'C', as in 'the Eastern Church'; when referring to the building itself, I use a small 'c'.

Jesus Christ

The word 'Christ' is essentially the same as 'Messiah'. Christ comes from the Greek word *Khristos*, and Messiah comes from the Hebrew word *Mashiach*, both of which translate as 'anointed' or 'the anointed one'. Although the names Jesus and Christ are virtually interchangeable when writing or speaking about Jesus, writers tend to use 'Jesus' when they are talking in terms of his humanity, and 'Christ' when talking in terms of his divinity. To be consistent, I have tended to stick to 'Jesus'.

The Virgin Mary

'The Blessed Virgin Mary' is the full title with which Catholics honour Jesus' mother. She can also be known simply as 'the Virgin'. Protestant Churches, which tend to place less emphasis on Mary's position, use these titles less often. To tread a middle path – and to save space – I refer to Mary simply as THE VIRGIN MARY.

Catholic / Roman Catholic

The word 'Catholic' denotes traditions or beliefs in the Western Church that originate in, or claim continuity with, the early Church. It therefore refers to practices that continue within many Churches, for example among Anglicans, and not only among Roman Catholics. For example, the form of service conducted in Roman Catholic churches and many Anglican churches is virtually indistinguishable, since both are based on traditions that originated in the early Church and which developed over the centuries. Those practices are 'Catholic'. I will be using the description 'Catholic' when referring to traditional teachings and customs in the Western Church, and the term 'Roman Catholic' to refer specifically to the Roman Catholic Church.

READING A CHURCH: PRELIMINARIES 1

How do you go about 'reading' a church? In some ways, it is easy. There are particular elements of the Christian story, ideas and history that appear again and again in the images found in churches. Understanding these gives a solid foundation for understanding the images themselves.

WHY READ A CHURCH?

Churches and cathedrals are packed with meaning. Outside, the spire points heavenwards, while carvings around the entrance announce the holiness of the space inside. All around, NUMBERS, COLOURS, the ANIMALS and PLANTS in the stonework, and the scenes in the stained glass, point to aspects of Christian teachings about God. In a number of senses, and to different degrees, churches were built to be read.

Churches can contain many images, but what is the point of them all? It is often said that images in older churches were meant for people who could not read, so that they could understand the Christian message as the educated did. This explanation of church imagery as 'the storybook of the illiterate' is good and democratic, and fits in well with the very principles that are its cause, but I am not sure it is true. There

✣

The doorway of the church of St Mary, Streatley, Berkshire.
and (above) *foliage on a capital in Lichfield Cathedral,*
Staffordshire.

are few, or no, images that can be understood without already knowing the story that they represent. The literate and the illiterate would have been equally familiar with the basics, and I do not believe that these images would have been any more useful for the peasant than for the king. In fact, the 'picture-book' pleasure to be had from the images is as good for the educated as the uneducated. It comes from the sense of sudden recognition, the satisfaction of the images sliding into place alongside the old, familiar stories.

The world of symbols is deep and rich and varied. True, many are rather less democratic. Roman or Greek words and letters carved in stone or painted on windows may have been understood only by the classically educated. These can suggest some hidden knowledge of God, exclusive to those who can interpret it, such as the clergy or the well-to-do.

Blythburgh Church, Blythburgh, Norfolk.

It is also important to remember that the world of symbols is not fixed. The symbols recorded here have certain generally accepted meanings. But those meanings have developed over centuries or even millennia, and there is every reason to suppose that their meanings will continue to develop. Objects have different resonances for different people at different times, and readers should take their experiences with them when 'reading' symbols. Take the BULRUSH, for example. This is a symbol of God's sustaining and saving power, derived from the Book of Job. But for me, bulrushes are a reminder of the great Essex reed beds that had to be traversed to get to the beach when I was a child and are connected, for me, with the confusing passage of life and the final promise of joy and light.

Turning to churches themselves, it is often said that we could, or even should, do without them. God is in the fields and in the woods, in the earth and in the wind, and is not contained within four walls. Many people feel closer to God on a walk in the park than in a building on a Sunday morning and

St Andrew's Old Church, Upleatham, near Cleveland, North Yorkshire. It has a Norman nave and a tower dating from 1684, and is one of the smallest churches in England.

early Christians often met to worship together at one another's homes. But churches were built to be Houses of God, emblematic of heaven on earth, made and decorated by men and women as expressions of love and reverence. And while they can of course be used for personal meditation, they are places of *communal* worship, of coming together. They are also – usually – very beautiful. We should not, however, forget that they are places of great spiritual power. Admiring a church for its exquisite beauty or history alone is like admiring a Monet for its frame.

CHRISTIAN THEOLOGY IN IMAGERY

Imagery was frequently put to use in illustrating or explaining points of Christian teaching, such as the 'dual nature' of Jesus or the triple importance of the central dogma in Eastern and Western Churches represented by THE TRINITY (page 138-9)

The creation of Eve, from Adam's rib, from the Nuremberg Bible. Animals in the Garden of Eden can be seen in the background, including a unicorn.

Christian teaching goes on to consider the relationship between God and man, and above all the sequence of sin, grace, and salvation. The Hebrew words signifying 'sin' in the Bible carry the notion of 'failure' or 'error', 'doing wrong' or 'revolt'. In Christian teaching, sin is brought into the world by humankind's moral and spiritual failure, and by disobedience to God. Adam and Eve, the first man and woman, were the first sinners, through disobeying God's command not to eat the fruit of the Tree of Knowledge of Good and Evil (see ADAM AND EVE, page 262). This 'Sin of Adam' led to the concept of 'Original Sin', which was most developed by the Christian teacher and theologian St Augustine (354–430). In Augustine's thought, when Adam first sinned he created a hereditary stain that would be carried by all humankind. Original Sin is therefore a passive state of being, rather than an active state of doing.

Salvation from sin comes through God's grace, and above all, in Christian thought, through Jesus. The root of the word 'grace' is Hebrew, and means 'bend down to', like a parent bending down to his or her child. Grace is the self-giving love of God, which is given regardless of whether the love is deserved by its object. For Christians, God's grace is most present in the suffering and death of Jesus, for the sake of all things.

Just how Jesus' sacrifice led to salvation remains the subject of theological debate. In the context of St Augustine's teaching about Original Sin, Jesus is the 'New Adam' who washed away the hereditary stain that was the legacy of Adam's disobedience. Jesus sacrificed himself as a blood offering, like a sacrificial lamb, and thereby 'paid' for the sins of humankind, so saving it from hell. Some theologians, though, have argued that ideas of heaven and hell, of rewards and punishments, are difficult to reconcile with biblical teachings about God's all-embracing love.

Tommaso Biazagi da Busla, Pietà (late 1400) in the Casa Cavasse Museum, Saluzzo, Italy.

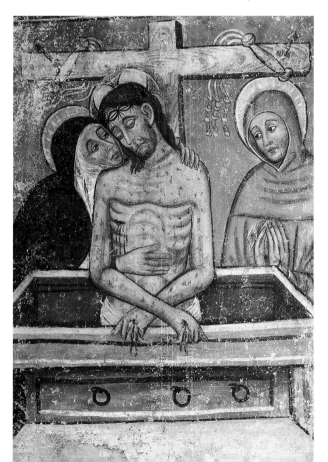

The Eucharist

Another manifestation of God is in THE EUCHARIST, also known as Holy Communion, the Mass, or the Lord's Supper. This is the central act of worship in the Western and Eastern Churches, and is referred to frequently in church imagery. The ceremony invokes the acts and words of Jesus at THE LAST SUPPER. Jesus broke bread and gave it to his disciples with the words 'Take, eat, this is my body'; he then took a cup of wine and gave it to the disciples with the words 'This is my blood of the covenant, poured out for many for the forgiveness of sins.'

There are three aspects of the Eucharist that are significant in church symbolism: the bread and the wine as Christ's body and blood; the Eucharist as a sacrifice; and the Eucharist as a shared meal in which everyone is invited to participate. The idea of the Eucharist as sacrifice is based on the very ancient understanding that there is some close relationship between Jesus' sacrifice on the cross and what takes place during the Eucharist. In some way, Jesus' sacrifice is perpetuated and reproduced in the ceremony.

Two Points of Church History

This is not a book about Church history, but history has had a great impact on the quantity and types of symbols and images found in individual Christian churches. There were two great earthquakes in Church history: the schism between the Eastern and Western Churches, and the Reformation.

By 'Western' Church, we mean the Roman Catholic and Protestant Churches. The 'Eastern' (or 'Orthodox') Church is a group of autonomous Churches that recognizes the honorary leadership of the Patriarch of Constantinople. The division between the two came about to a large part through historical accident. In the fifth century, the Western part of the Roman Empire was overrun by barbarian hordes, and the Pope, the head of the Church in Rome, came to take on much of the vanquished Emperor's authority. But in the East the former Roman Empire, now often called the Byzantine Empire, continued for another thousand years. It had its capital in Constantinople and the Patriarch there emerged as head of the Byzantine Church. Minor differences in ritual and teaching led to tensions that culminated in 1054 with the Pope and Patriarch excommunicating one another. Mutual non-recognition continued for several hundred years.

Stone carving on the tympanum of the church of
St Pierre de Moissac, France.

The impact of the schism for our purposes is that the Church of the East and the Church of the West developed different traditions in imagery and symbolism. Just one example of this is that the Eastern Church does not generally identify saints by the instruments of their martyrdom, as the Western Church often does. Moreover, the Eastern Church developed the use and veneration of icons. The 'Byzantine Guide to Painting', an ancient work which gives detailed guidance as to how Christian subjects should be portrayed, has largely been adhered to in decoding these formal paintings.

The Reformation occurred in the sixteenth century. The Western Church had become, in the eyes of its critics, spiritually bankrupt. Its officials were considered bloated and corrupt, concerned with their own wealth and power rather than the well-being of the people. Some practices attracted particular criticism, such as the sale of indulgences ('official' forgiveness for acts committed or not yet committed, in return for a fee), the veneration of relics, clergy who were absent from their churches, and nepotism in Church appointments.

The Church had seen a number of movements towards reform – for example, that led by ST FRANCIS OF ASSISI – but this time the critics struck at the Church's teachings themselves. There were a number of different voices in what became the Protestant Churches, but broadly speaking they emphasized the importance of reconciliation with God through faith and God's grace, as opposed to actions such as doing good deeds or buying indulgences; the importance of the authority of scripture, rather than tradition; they had different views on the nature of THE EUCHARIST, but did not accept that the bread and the wine were transformed into the body and blood of Christ during the ceremony, as the Roman Catholic Church taught; and they objected to the degree of veneration that had been allowed to the saints, and THE VIRGIN MARY in particular.

These objections led to the creation of the Protestant Churches, and a number of important denominations such as Lutheranism, Calvinism, and Presbyterianism soon sprang up.

The Crowning of Mary as Queen of Heaven by God the Father and God the Son, at the Monastery Church Museum, Rattenburg, Austria.

A banner depicting a chalice with angels at the church of St Anne, Buxton, Derbyshire.

Although it was not a Protestant movement as such, in England Henry VIII rejected the authority of the Pope and established the Anglican Church. The Roman Catholic Church in the meantime engaged in what became known as the Counter-Reformation. Much-needed internal reform went hand in hand with an emphasis on the beliefs and devotional subjects that were under attack, such as the life of ST PETER, or the real presence of Christ in the Eucharist. Spain and Italy became particular centres of Counter-Reformation activity.

The Reformation had equal and opposite effects in church art. In Protestant churches buildings tended to be plainer and less decorated. In some areas, iconoclasm raged, with

Protestants smashing imagery in churches, particularly of the Virgin Mary and the saints. Conversely, in the Roman Catholic Church imagery and symbolism became even more emphasized and elaborate. Over time, these distinctions would blur in some places. For example, in the nineteenth century, some in the Anglican Church championed the imagery and decoration of the medieval churches and a renaissance began in the use of images and symbols, complete with some references to extra-biblical sources.

A carving of Noah's Ark in a stone font. The Ark came to be a symbol of the Church.

Sources

The most common source of the images described in this book is, of course, the Bible. The Bible is a collection of texts that the Christian Church has acknowledged as being authoritative in their revelation of God. It comprises sixty-six books written over hundreds of years in an array of literary styles – historical narratives, folk tales, poetry, hymns, letters, and visions. The unifying thread is the story of God revealing himself to, and saving, the world. This passes from God's intimate relationship with the first man and woman in the Book of Genesis, through the story of the liberation of the Israelites from slavery in the Book of Exodus, messages from God in the books of the prophets, hymns to God in the Psalms, to the teachings, death, and resurrection of Jesus in the

Gospels, the teachings in the letters of ST PAUL and other early Christians, and concluding in a vision of the end of the world, in the final Book of Revelation.

But the Bible is not the only written source of imagery. Many images are derived from texts described as apocryphal, which means that they are in some way associated with, but not always accepted into, the official canon. Some of these are ancient Hebrew stories that did not make it into the Old Testament, others are post-resurrection stories, written after the four biblical Gospels, which claimed to tell further stories of Jesus' life.

Over time, the public also developed a passion for tales of the disciples, and stories of the saints, many of which found their way into church imagery (the most famous collection of these tales is a medieval work called *The Golden Legend*). Moreover, as men and women built and decorated churches, they did not feel constrained to fit inside a textual tradition. They borrowed from the natural world, making analogies between nature and the Christian story, such as the low-growing VIOLET becoming a symbol of humility; they co-opted legends and fairy stories into the Christian message, such as tales of the UNICORN and the BASILISK; and they were influenced by pre-Christian traditions, such as the CROSS as a symbol of life.

Oyrarbaki Church, Esturoy on the Faroe Islands.

CHURCH 2
ARCHITECTURE

BANDS OF SACREDNESS

Places of worship are arranged into spaces with increasing degrees of holiness. At the time of Jesus, the Temple of Herod the Great in Jerusalem was arranged in just this way. The outermost part of the precincts was the Court of the Gentiles, open to Jew and non-Jew alike. A more sacred inner court, into which only Jews were allowed, led to two further courtyards, the Court of the Women and the Court of Israel. Nearer still to the Temple was the Court of Priests, into which only priests were allowed. The Temple itself was divided into the outer vestibule and the NAVE, the area where much of the Temple's ritual took place. Within this, separated by a curtain, stood the inner sanctuary, the 'holy of holies', the dwelling-place of God.

Churches too contain these degrees of sanctity, of spaces separated within spaces. The process starts at the wall of the CHURCHYARD. Medieval 'sanctuary', the area within which a criminal could not be arrested, started at the border of the church grounds. Next comes the church building itself. The building may be marked out as containing a holy space by the CROSS standing on its spire (when a church is put out of

⁎

The magnificent Chichester Cathedral which was dedicated by Bishop Ralph Luffa in 1108, and (above) a detail from a stained-glass window at Moorside Church, Kirby, Yorkshire.

service, it is formally deconsecrated, and the cross is removed). The main body of the church, the nave, is the area where the congregation takes part in the service. Beyond this lies the chancel, usually separated from the nave by a step and/or ARCH, and often set up with choir stalls. Beyond the chancel is the sanctuary, again often separated from the chancel by a step and arch and ALTAR rail, within which only the priests and their attendants are allowed. Within the sanctuary is the altar. In Catholic churches, standing on or behind the altar is a small space of even greater holiness, the TABERNACLE. It is the church's own holy of holies.

But an important difference in Christian thought between the divisions of church and temple is that whereas in the temple the holy of holies could only be approached by the high priest, in a church it is the resting place of a meal that can be shared by all believers, and can be approached (in the Western Church) by the whole of the congregation. This joining together of God and humankind is an important aspect of Christian teaching, illustrated in a striking way in Matthew's Gospel. MATTHEW says that when Jesus died, the curtain that separated the holy of holies from the rest of the Temple was torn in two. One meaning of this story is that the death of Jesus destroyed the division between God and humankind.

ORIENTATION

Before the destruction of Herod's Temple in AD 70, there were few 'dedicated' synagogue buildings. The Temple in Jerusalem was the focus of religious life, and meetings away from the Temple took place in private homes or public halls (the word synagogue means 'gathering together'). The early Church followed the same practice. But when building did begin, it soon developed a common pattern.

To begin with, almost universal customs developed as to direction. East and south are the honoured sides, north and west less favoured. Facing eastwards for worship, in the direction that the sun rises, is a practice that is probably pre-Christian, and there are a number of biblical references to God

⟊

Southwell Minster, Southwell, Nottinghamshire. One of England's lesser-known cathedrals, construction of the present building was begun in 1108 and work continued for the next 200 years.

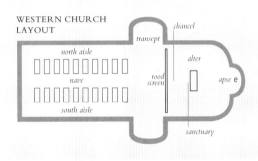

WESTERN CHURCH LAYOUT

chancel
transept
north aisle
nave
rood screen
south aisle
alter
apse e
sanctuary

in the east (for example, 'the glory of the Lord was coming from the east', Ezekiel 43:2). The west may also have had a negative linguistic association, since the Latin *occidere*, 'to kill', was associated with the Occident, to the west. You will find that the longitudinal axis of most churches is therefore west–east, with the entrance on the west side and the altar on the east (I say 'most' because this is simply a common practice; there is no fixed rule). As the congregation worships it is usually facing eastwards, and images that express Christian hope are often deployed in the east window. The west side, on the other hand, was considered the best place for 'Doom' paintings of THE LAST JUDGEMENT. In much the same way, in the northern hemisphere the warm, light south was preferred to the dark north, and you will find that the entrances to churches, and the more favoured burial sites, are on the southern side. As a final directional point, the right-hand side was seen as good, while the left was bad (the Latin word for left, *sinister*, now means 'suggestive of evil').

As you approach a settlement you may well see the church first, standing on raised ground. For churches with the very oldest foundation, this may be because they were placed on a raised site with some religious, pre-Christian significance. It was Church policy to absorb, rather than destroy, the sites of pagan worship. In some churchyards ancient stones stand, marked with a cross to signify their transformation from a pagan to a Christian point of worship, or they may have been incorporated into the churchyard cross, gateposts, or the fabric of the church. The more prosaic explanation for raised ground is that, as graveyards filled with bodies, the ground increased in height. Also, in lower-lying areas, churches were put on raised ground to stop them flooding.

LYCHGATES

You may find a LYCHGATE at the entrance to some English churchyards This small shelter over the entrance gate, often covering a central stone platform and perhaps seats on either side, was designed to act as a shelter for coffins and pallbearers before they came into the church for a funeral. The name comes from *lic*, an Old English word for corpse, and the pallbearers would rest the coffin on the stone platform as they waited on the seats for the priest presiding over the funeral to come out of the church to meet the coffin. There was a legal reason for this, in that the cleric needed to receive the legal certificate for burial from the dead man's relatives outside the church. Over time, though, this has come to be seen as a mark of respect for the deceased. The priest meets the coffin at the entrance of the CHURCHYARD, before conducting it into the church.

✛

The lychgate at the church of St Mawnan, Mawnan, near Falmouth, Cornwall. The inscription is in Old Cornish and reads: 'It is good for me to be nigh to God'.

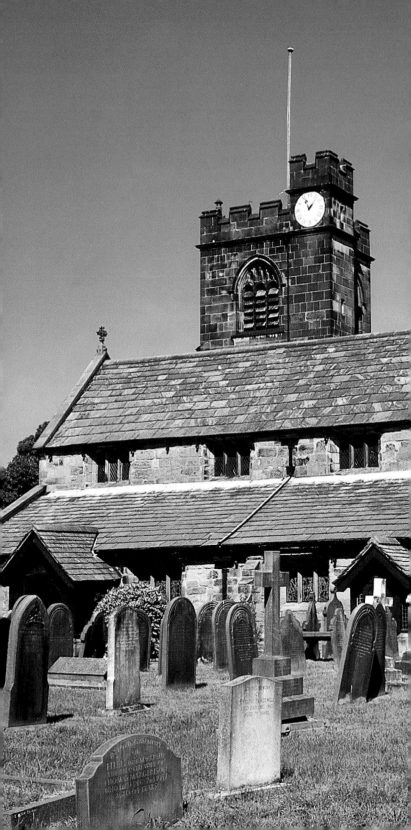

THE CHURCHYARD

CHURCHYARDS are almost invariably used as graveyards. Graves face east because this was the 'honourable' direction: Christians adopted the old Jewish custom of burying the dead with their feet towards the rising sun, as a sign of hope. There was also a belief that when Jesus returned to earth to rule over a new kingdom, the faithful would rise up bodily from their graves. It was believed that Jesus would return to Jerusalem, and therefore Christians living west of Israel wanted to face eastwards, so that they were facing the right way at the moment of his return. A similar belief in some Jewish thought is that the Messiah will enter Jerusalem through the Golden Gate, a now sealed gate that leads onto Temple Mount and the Dome of the Rock. This belief has caused the graveyard that looks towards the Golden Gate to be the most sought-after burial site in Israel.

The south side of the church was preferred for burials and therefore tends to be higher. The ground on the north side was sometimes used for the burial of suicides, criminals, and infants who had not been baptized. Some rebelled against this arrangement, though: a gravestone at Epworth in Lincolnshire reads, 'That I might longer undisturbed abide/I choos'd to be laid on this Northern side'. This arrangement of the churchyard and the preference for the south explains why churches tend to be placed on the north end of the churchyard, with the entrance facing south. It allows more space for burials and a longer entrance-path, and has the added bonus of reminding visitors of the dead person, as they pass by their gravestone.

Some old churchyards contain a large CROSS. This marks the point where the priest would sometimes preach in the open air. In the days when tombstones were less common, the churchyard cross also served as a single memorial for all of the dead buried there.

✢

The church of St Leonard-the-Less, Samlesbury, near Preston, Lancashire, which was consecrated in 1196.

GARGOYLES are highly decorated drainage pipes designed to throw rainwater clear of the church walls through a projecting spout concealed in the throat of a monstrous being or fantastic shape. The word comes from the Latin *gurgulio*, meaning throat, a root shared with the word 'gargle'. Beautifully carved, they were sometimes installed simply for their own sake. There are symbolic interpretations of them, for example that gargoyles were intended to scare away the Devil, or that they make a symbolic contrast between the bedevilled world outside the walls of the church and the sanctuary within. But you have to be suspicious of symbolism in relation to gargoyles, since above all they gave opportunity for expression by local carvers, as their often fabulous work – terrifying, comic, bawdy, macabre, and rarely very 'holy' – attests.

❖

Above *A gargoyle on the church of St Anne and St Laurence, Elmstead, Essex and* (right) *another example, this time on Chichester Cathedral.*

PORCHES & DOORS

PORCHES

Church PORCHES were an obvious place for secular business, and had important community functions. In England, they sometimes contained an ALTAR at which legally binding contracts could be sworn – few of these altars survive, but look out for remnants of them, such as a niche for a statue or an irregular arrangement of the stone benches or doors. If the porch was large enough, it could be used for dispensing justice (in the churches of Alrewas and Yoxall in Staffordshire, courts were held until the nineteenth century), while in a room above the porch, schooling would take place. In the Middle Ages couples about to be married were met at the porch and asked for their consent before proceeding inside for the ceremony.

DOORS

DOORWAYS often feature references to Jesus: you may find sculptures of Jesus sitting in majesty, a Virgin and child, a LAMB OF GOD or a CRUCIFIXION over or around the doorway. Jesus' parable of the wise and foolish virgins (Matthew 25: 1-13). is a popular image on the doors themselves. Before a wedding feast, the wise virgins prepared by making sure their lamps were full of oil and trimmed. The foolish virgins did not, so that when the bridegroom suddenly arrived at the feast, they were unprepared and he shut the door on them. The foolish virgins may be shown holding their lamps upside down to show their emptiness.

Heavy and elaborate handles on the entrance door may derive from the use of churches as a place of sanctuary to fugitives. A fugitive was, in principle, safe from capture if he or she claimed sanctuary in a church. An unproved theory is that once a person had grasped the handle, he or she could not be removed without breaking sanctuary. The Constable of Arundel was compelled to do penance for having taken a thief who was holding on to the door handle of Arundel church.

✢

The Norman portal at the church of St Mary and St David, Kilpeck,
Herefordshire. The tympanum contains a Tree of Life. Snakes,
'Welsh Warriors', and the Green Man can be seen on the pillars.

INSIDE A **3** CHURCH

The inside of a church is packed with meaning. There is specific relevance in the layout: the aisle that draws you to the ALTAR, with its ranks of pews on either side, is the gangway of a ship carrying worshippers to God; the altar, the holy heart of the building, is contained in a separated and sacred space; all around, NUMBERS, COLOURS, the ANIMALS and PLANTS in the stonework, and the scenes in the paintings and the stained glass all point to aspects of Christian teaching about God.

1	East Window	11	Chancel
2	Cross	12	Lady chapel
3	Hymn board	13	Chancel step
4	Crucifix	14	Pews
5	Lectern	15	Nave
6	Altar	16	Memorial brass
7	Choir pews	17	Font
8	Pulpit		
9	Organ		
10	Altar rails		

✤

Virtually every part of the church of St Giles, Cheadle, Staffordshire, including these stalls, or sedilia, is highly decorated and painted. The lavish design was the work of Augustin Pugin (1812-52).

Stoups & Fonts

Stoups

In some, especially Roman Catholic, churches, there is a STOUP by the entrance, a recessed bowl of stone or metal containing holy (blessed) water. Entrants to the church dip their fingers in the water and cross themselves with it. The stoup is a descendant of Jewish customs of ritual washing of the hands, face, and sometimes feet. These customs were carried into the earliest churches, which placed a fountain at the entrance for washing; over time it was felt that size did not matter, since the washing was purely symbolic, and so the fountain became the stoup. The stoup is therefore used to express the person's wish to be spiritually clean before entering the church building.

Fonts

The FONT is usually placed at the rear of the church, near the start of the central aisle. Since the central aisle represents the Christian's journey through life towards God, it was thought appropriate that the font should be placed at the symbolic start of the journey. The font is used for baptism – ST JOHN THE BAPTIST baptized those that heard his message, and baptized Jesus himself. Baptism is one of the seven Sacraments, and signifies a washing clean of the participants. It is also a presentation ceremony, a welcoming of the individual into the community.

Fonts may be lidded, and the lids themselves range from simple covers to grand architectural confections (at Ullaford in Suffolk the cover is an eighteen-foot spire). Lids were used because the water was blessed on Easter day and then left there for later use (fonts therefore had to be impermeable in the long term as well as the short, which is why some are lined with lead). The holy water had to be protected from dirt and dust, and also from theft for use in charms and magical rituals. In England covers became compulsory from 1236, although nowadays water used in baptism is blessed on the day.

❖

The fifteenth-century octagonal font at the church of St Mary Magdalene, Newark, Nottinghamshire. There are sixteen figures pictured around the plinth below, which were restored in 1660.

✤ NAVES, COLUMNS & ARCHES

NAVE

The central area of a church, the main aisle flanked by rows of pews, is known as the NAVE. It is the space for the laity, the congregation. The word comes from the Latin *navis*, meaning ship, the root of the English word 'navigation'. The association of the church with a ship, and the congregation as passengers in the ship, indicates the priests and people travelling together towards God. Pews are a fairly modern invention. Previously the congregation would stand (even mill about), although sometimes stone seats can be seen around the base of columns or against the walls, for use by the infirm (this was the origin of the expression 'the weakest to the wall'). Pews began to be installed in northern Europe after the Reformation, when an emphasis on the importance of sermons developed. These sermons were often very lengthy, and the congregation needed to rest its weary legs.

COLUMNS

The NAVE may be flanked by COLUMNS, which draw the eye forward towards the altar. Columns resonate with ancient pagan beliefs and practices. First, they are like trees. The first columns would have been made of wood, hewn out of single tree-trunks. The shape of the earliest known stone columns suggests mimicry by the carvers of these trunks, and the leafy decoration at the tops of some columns reinforces the connection. The central space of a church flanked with columns is therefore like the sacred groves in which our ancestors worshipped. Secondly, columns are akin to human figures, like ancient standing stones. Erect stones have long been used to represent people, and human names can be attached to them ('the Seven Maidens', 'the Long Man'). In a church the columns stand like these stones, their human shape flanking the congregation. The tops of the columns may fly into buttresses, like arms raised in perpetual praise to God. Sites

✤

Differing styles of pillars and arches. Columns flanking the central space of a church are reminiscent of tree trunks, and the arches may suggest hands clasped together in worship.

such as Stonehenge have been compared to cathedrals, but it may be that the analogy should be reversed: churches are our Stonehenge.

Doric

The periods of architecture enjoy different styles of columns, but it is columns from the Greek and Roman traditions that have particular symbolic significance. Classical Greek architecture was organized into three 'orders': Doric, Ionic, and Corinthian. Each order had a different set of principles that determined the order of shapes and spatial relationships between the parts, and each had its own distinctive columns. Doric columns tend to be plain, with simple rounded heads, or capitals, and are shorter and thicker than the later versions. The capitals of Ionic columns, which are taller and more

Ionic

Corinthian

slender than Doric columns, look like opposing scrolls. Corinthian columns are topped with an arrangement of pointed acanthus leaves, which the Greeks viewed as having a special beauty. Roman architecture adopted these orders and added its own, including the Composite order, in which columns were topped with a fusion of the Ionic curls and the Corinthian leaves, to refer both to wisdom and to beauty.

Plain, sturdy Doric columns were associated with masculinity and strength, while graceful, slender Ionic columns were associated with the feminine, scholarship, and wisdom. Therefore, Doric columns tend to be used in churches dedicated to male saints, Ionic in churches for female saints. Corinthian columns, which were thought to be possessed of particular beauty, were used in honour of THE VIRGIN MARY. Within a church building, different styles of columns can be used in different places, depending on the saints in the locality. For example, small Corinthian columns sometimes frame images of Mary.

⊹

The simple arrangement of columns and arches here forms a stately rhythm along the nave.

ARCHES

ARCHES have been interpreted symbolically as being like hands clasped in prayer, or arms thrown up in worship of God. A happy symbolic meaning relates to marriage. Couples are usually married under the chancel arch, which divides the chancel from the NAVE. Michelangelo defined an arch as two powerful forces that meet at their weakest point to make a stronger whole – a metaphor that seems good for marriage, too.

Some arches in much larger churches built in the classical tradition are 'triumphal', characterized by their great size and thickness, and by a rounded arch. Triumphal arches were originally freestanding, built by Roman Emperors to march beneath with their army, in celebration of an important victory. They were resurrected in more recent times, modern examples being the Arc de Triomphe in Paris and Marble Arch in London. When incorporated into church building, for example in the entrance, they symbolize the victory of Jesus. The priest and congregation as they pass beneath them are imitating the triumphant victory marches of the emperors.

The term 'triumphal arch' also refers to the wall above the arch that separates the nave from the chancel, and which is sometimes decorated with mosaics.

CEILINGS & DOMES

The church is a symbol of heaven, of the world as it should and could be. Some churches therefore refuse to see themselves as enclosed buildings – they are a world-within-a-world. The CEILING, particularly that of the chancel, or the sanctuary, can be painted to look like the heavens, as if the whole world is contained within the walls of the church. There may be clouds, or a night sky dotted with stars, or angels, or Jesus sitting in majesty in heaven. If there is not enough space to represent these images on the flat surfaces between the vaults, they are sometimes carved on the roof bosses. Virtually the only images of THE CORONATION OF THE VIRGIN left in English churches are those that appear on roof bosses. The images are high on the bosses because the coronation took place in heaven, and their inaccessibility saved them from the iconoclasts of the Reformation.

The meeting of a rounded dome with a square-walled building, which is a particularly common template of the buildings of the Eastern Church, has theological meaning as well. The DOME, which represents heaven, atop a walled box, which represents earth (like a square or cube – see NUMBERS and SHAPES, pages 114-117), is meant to symbolize the descent of heaven to earth in the person of Jesus, and in THE EUCHARIST. The chief model for church building in the Eastern Church is Hagia Sofia in Constantinople (modern-day Istanbul), in which a vast dome sits on an early Christian basilica.

✣

The great dome of the church of St Mary, Mosta, Malta, also known as the Rotunda, and (above) *the magnificent vaulted ceiling of Norwich Cathedral.*

INSIDE A CHURCH

47

LECTURNS & PULPITS

LECTERN

The LECTERN, on which the Bible rests for reading during services, is placed near the division between the chancel and the NAVE. It is usually in the shape of an EAGLE, with the Bible resting on its outspread wings, although there are also instances of lecterns in the shape of a PELICAN. The eagle was thought to be able to look unflinchingly into the heart of the sun; in the same way, the words from the Bible are an unflinching revelation of God. The pelican was said in medieval bestiaries to peck at its breast in order to feed its young with its own blood; its selflessness is seen as a direct analogy with Jesus' sacrifice.

PULPIT

PULPITS, from which sermons are delivered to the congregation, were introduced into Western churches in around the fourteenth century. Since they are the focus for teaching, images of THE FOUR EVANGELISTS or the four Latin Doctors are sometimes found carved into them.

✥

An ornate lectern and (right) *a highly decorated wooden pulpit in a Norwegian church. The tradition of such intricate wood-carving in Scandinavia dates back to the pre-Christian era.*

Screens & Lady Chapels

SCREENS

The SCREEN stands between the chancel and the NAVE in Eastern churches. It is decorated with icons – formal and revered paintings of Jesus, THE VIRGIN MARY and the saints - and is pierced by three DOORS. The central, or royal, door leads to the ALTAR; the prothesis, which leads to the area where THE EUCHARIST is prepared, is on the left; and the diaconicaon, on the right, leads to the space where the sacred vessels are kept and cleaned, and books and vestments stored.

In some Western churches, particularly in some parts of England, a 'rood screen' can stand dividing the nave from the chancel. 'Rood' is an Anglo-Saxon word meaning 'cross', and the rood screen can be topped with a tall cross, often flanked by statues of the Virgin Mary and ST JOHN (both of whom were present at THE CRUCIFIXION).

Originally built to keep people (and animals) out of the chancel, the rood screen could be topped with a rood loft, a narrow gallery from which prayers could be said and hymns sung, especially at major feast-days. Most rood lofts were pulled down at the time of the Reformation, and in older churches a doorway at the entrance to the chancel, with steps leading to another doorway higher up (apparently leading nowhere), is where the rood loft was accessed. Many rood screens were destroyed at the same time, although some have survived, and in England some were installed during the Victorian fashion for church architecture in a medieval style.

LADY CHAPEL

Many churches, particularly large churches dating from before the Reformation, include a small LADY CHAPEL. The chapel is dedicated to, and will contain images of, THE VIRGIN MARY. Lady chapels tend to be used for services for smaller congregations (for example, mid-week services), and for the spillover of people when very large congregations are present.

⁕

The rood screen in the church of St Giles, Cheadle, Staffordshire. Designed by Augustus Pugin (1812–52), St Giles is one of the greatest examples of the Gothic Revival style.

ALTAR & TABERNACLE

The ALTAR is the holy heart of the church. It has two principal reference points. First, it is a sacrificial altar. At the time of Jesus' ministry, animal sacrifice as atonement for sin, performed on an altar, was normal Jewish ritual. Christian writers from ST PAUL onwards saw Jesus as having been like a sacrificial LAMB in his CRUCIFIXION and death. Secondly, it is a table for a communal meal, again remembering and repeating THE LAST SUPPER, when Jesus shared a meal with his disciples. These threads of sacrifice and a shared meal are joined in THE EUCHARIST. Recently, the altars in some churches have migrated. In the early 1960s, the Roman Catholic Church changed the practice of having the priest celebrate the Eucharist with his back to the congregation. Instead, the priest would stand behind the altar and face the people, creating a sense of dialogue and equality between the two. The purpose being to emphasize the sharing of the ceremony, and the equality of the participants before God.

A candle can hang before the altar. A white candle shows that 'reserved sacrament' (that is, bread and wine that was blessed but not consumed during the Eucharist) is present in the TABERNACLE. Some churches keep a candle in a red lamp alight as a perpetual flame, to symbolize the continual presence of God. It remembers the menorah, the seven-branched lamp that God commanded the Israelites to burn before the altar during THE EXODUS. The tabernacle is a decorated box which stands on or behind the altar in Catholic churches.

The name is the same as that used for the tent, in effect a portable temple, that the Israelites were commanded by God to construct and carry with them during the Exodus. Worship took place in the tabernacle, and the Ark of the Covenant, which contained the stones bearing THE TEN COMMANDMENTS, was placed there. The church tabernacle, used to store the bread (the metaphorical body of Jesus) for the ceremony of the Eucharist, becomes therefore the heart of the church.

✣

A lithograph by H. C. Maguire for The Glossary of Ecclesiastical Ornament and Costume *by Augustus Pugin (1844).*

Symbols 4

A SYMBOL is something that represents or stands for something else. There are three characteristics of symbols that make them as important today as they have ever been. Firstly, symbols can express concepts that language alone cannot. That is especially the case for mystical concepts, which, almost by definition, we can only approach and not completely grasp. But we *can* understand, and accept, a *symbol* of those concepts. In fact, given that a symbol may be trying to express the inexpressible, it could be as perfect an understanding of the concept as we can ever achieve. Secondly, symbols can help to bridge gaps between the Eastern and Western Churches where language is simply too trouble-making. Christians can all agree that a triangle expresses THE TRINITY. Thirdly, a symbol may have the power to touch us at a depth that a wordy exposition does not. The language of symbols is an old one, some of it rooted in practices and ideas that predate Christianity. Although their context may point to one interpretation over another, a single symbol can have multiple, even contradictory meanings. These meanings can inform and colour one another. Deep and rich and varied, they can connect with us in a way that we barely understand.

⁜

General nature scene; church of St Gregory, Great Vale of Lune near Sedburgh, Cumbria, and (above) *Christ carries the cross towards Calvary.*

CROSSES, CRUCIFIXES
& HALOS

The CROSS is Christianity's most important symbol, although its meaning in churches can be complex. Depending on how they are portrayed or displayed, crosses can evoke sacrifice and death, or love and hope.

Greek cross with six unequal branches

The sign of the cross is a spiritual symbol that predates Christianity. Two of the earliest forms with spiritual significance are the SWASTIKA in India and the Orient, and the ankh, or ansa, in ancient Egypt. The swastika represented sacred fire and fruitfulness, and was attributed to the goddess Maia, who personified productive powers. The ankh was held by Sekhet, the lion-headed goddess of vengeance and conquest, but it became a hieroglyphic sign for life, or the living. It is striking that both of these cross-shaped symbols, developed so far apart, were life-affirming.

The cross was not a symbol of the earliest Christians, who preferred the ANCHOR, FISH, or CHI RHO. THE CRUCIFIXION was not a symbol for the early Church. It was only over time that Christians began to think through the implications and meanings of the crucifixion, and to glorify the cross. It seems, though, that Jesus – who predicted his own death by crucifixion – always understood the cross's positive, redemptive significance.

✥

The design of a wheel-head cross incorporates a circle, possibly representing a crown, a halo, rays of light or the circle of eternity.
Right, A processional cross from St Martin's, Worle, Somerset.

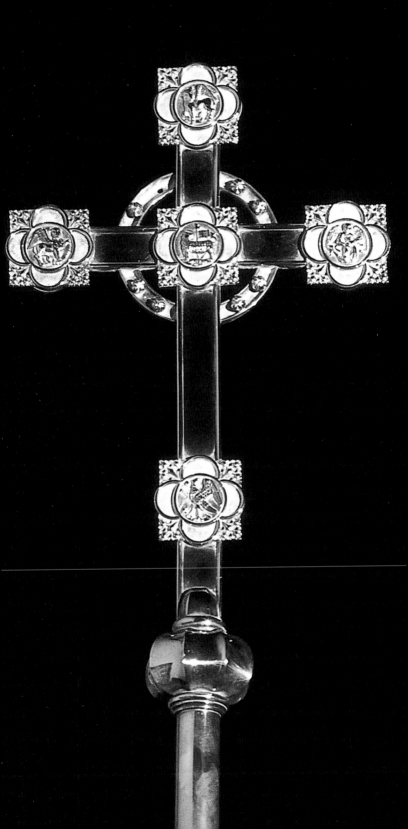

CROSSES & CRUCIFIXES

THE EMPTY CROSS

The cross shown is the plain or 'EMPTY' CROSS, a cross without the figure of Jesus hanging on it. The empty cross is an instrument of torture that has been defeated, from which the victim has walked away. In Christian teaching, Jesus died on the cross but he rose again, defying the cross's power – 'O death, where is thy sting!' The empty cross is therefore an image of God's power, and of hope. It is hope that shines through the story of THE CRUCIFIXION – the utter helplessness of Jesus on the cross, with the promise of his teachings and vision seeming to end in agonizing death, but in the end giving way to new life and glory.

THE CROSS-ANCHOR

The message of hope is also symbolized by the CROSS-ANCHOR – an anchor in which the upper beam forms the shape of a cross. Like the cross, the anchor was a symbol before the Christian period. Since they held ships safely in place, anchors were ancient symbols of safety, and so of hope. It may have been adopted by the early Christians as a covert symbol. In Christian terms, anchors are specifically a symbol of the hope of salvation and of eternal life, which explains why they are found on many early Christian graves.

CRUCIFIXES OF JESUS' TRIUMPH

CRUCIFIXES are crosses to which the body of Jesus is fixed, or superimposed. On some, Jesus is shown with his arms outstretched, dressed in a long, seamless tunic (a colobium or alb) and wearing a HALO and gold crown in kingly, or priestly dress. His hands may show him in the act of blessing the onlookers (with two fingers extended), or the palms may be

⁂

Detail of a stained-glass window depicting the Crucifixion at the church of All Saints, Shelley, West Yorkshire. Jesus' head hangs to the right (considered to be the 'good' side).

open, in an attitude of openness and embrace (in the words of the Eucharistic prayer, used during THE EUCHARIST, 'he opened wide his arms for us upon the cross'). This is Jesus triumphant, defeating the cross but also glorifying it. Historically, the image was most popular between the sixth and thirteenth centuries, when artists preferred not to strip Jesus of his clothes.

CRUCIFIXES OF JESUS' SUFFERING

From around the thirteenth century, CRUCIFIXES increasingly memorialized Jesus' suffering and death. Jesus is shown with his head to one side (the convention is for the head to hang to the 'good' right), and he is shown as having just died. He is wearing the crown of thorns, and is nailed through the palms of his hands, with a single nail piercing his crossed feet, to give a devotional pose. A cut just below the ribs shows where Jesus was speared as he hung on the cross.

The reality of crucifixion is appalling. Scourging always preceded it, following which the condemned man had to carry his own, tremendously heavy, CROSS (or at least the cross-beam) to the place of execution. The victim was stripped naked. Long nails were then driven, not through the palms of the hands, but through the wrist bones. Without this arrangement, the victim's weight would have caused the nails to simply rip through his flesh. For the same reason, nails may have been driven just below and behind each ankle, one on each side of the central beam of the cross, rather than through the middle of the feet. Many crucifixes include a small footrest with this in mind, although in reality a small central prop, shaped like a rhino horn, often acted as a seat to give the victim support. The downward pull of the body would have caused a slow suffocation. The lungs would gradually fill with fluid and victims could hang in agony for days. It was against Jewish law for a person to remain crucified over the Sabbath, and so on Friday afternoon if a victim was still alive his legs would be broken, finally killing him with the shock, before he was taken down.

✛

The south porch at the twelfth-century apsidal church of St Michael and All Angels, Copford, near Colchester, Essex.

SHAPES OF CROSSES

CELTIC

The CELTIC or wheel-head cross incorporates a circle. The origin and symbolism of this is not known, although the wheel has been thought to represent a crown, a HALO, rays of light, or the circle of eternity. Its popularity may simply derive from its additional strength.

EASTER

The EASTER CROSS is garlanded by flowers (especially the LILY, although they are nowadays seen as often with spring-time daffodils), symbolizing new life.

GRADED

The GRADED CROSS has three steps leading up to it, symbolic (from the base) of faith, hope, and love.

PAPAL

The PAPAL CROSS, which is carried before the Pope, has three bars, like the Pope's triple crown, or the inscription (INRI), crossbar, and foot-rest.

PASSION

A cross that has its ends coming to points is the PASSION CROSS, as the points represent the wounds of Jesus.

PATRIARCHAL

The PATRIARCHAL CROSS of the Eastern Church has two bars, for the inscription and crossbar.

SWASTIKA

The SWASTIKA appears fairly frequently on old Christian monuments in Rome, but the appalling associations of the last century mean that it is now little seen elsewhere.

✢

Celtic or wheel-head cross, with elaborate Celtic designs.
This one is at Highgate Cemetery
in north London.

Tau

In Western Europe the cross usually has the vertical extending above the cross-beam. Sometimes, though, the cross is shown shaped like the letter T, reflecting a debate in the early Church on the proper shape of the cross. A Y-shape is less common, but appears in some northern European churches.

Triumph

A cross sitting on a globe (a globe is sometimes placed under the cross on a church spire) is the CROSS OF TRIUMPH, and symbolizes victory over the whole world.

The Use of Particular Crosses

ALTAR crosses have swung in and out of fashion over the centuries. Protestant and Roman Catholic Churches diverged in their practices at the Reformation: reformers tended to be against ornamentation of any kind; conversely, Roman Catholics made the altar cross a permanent fixture and increasingly used crucifixes instead of the plain crosses of before. Nowadays, Roman Catholic churches keep a CRUCIFIX on the altar, guarded by at least two candlesticks. The processional cross stands on a pole, and is often kept by the altar or near it on its own stand.

Look out for consecration crosses. These mark the points on the walls where a church was anointed when it was consecrated. This ritual is intended to sanctify the building and dedicate it to God. It therefore separates it from the 'ordinary' space outside, and differentiates it from other buildings. The consecrating bishop makes twelve signs of the cross, three on each wall. These spots are marked in a permanent way, in paint or with a stone or metal cross (perishable crosses, such as those made from wood, are not allowed in the Roman Catholic Church). Each is marked with holy oil and a candle placed under it. The crosses should never be removed, because they are proof that the space within the four walls has been consecrated. Some churches have the same spots on their outer walls.

✣

A Crucifix of Jesus' triumph on the exterior of Bradford Cathedral, West Yorkshire. The hand of God the Father reaches downwards.

✠ THE STATIONS OF THE CROSS

The 'STATIONS OF THE CROSS' (also the Via Crucis, the 'Way of the Cross', and the Via Dolorosa, the 'Way of Sorrow') are arrayed as tableaux, small reliefs or paintings around the walls of some churches and enable Christians to perform their own meditative 'pilgrimage' in the footsteps of Jesus. The number of stations is now a fairly fixed canon, but there are and have been variations, with the number of scenes increasing to as many as thirty-one. The stations nowadays show:

1   JESUS CONDEMNED TO BE CRUCIFIED;
2   JESUS TAKING UP THE CROSS;
3   JESUS FALLING UNDER THE WEIGHT OF THE CROSS
    (THE FIRST FALL);
4   JESUS MEETING THE VIRGIN MARY;
5   SIMON OF CYRENE BEING FORCED TO CARRY THE
    CROSS, IN PLACE OF JESUS;
6   ST VERONICA WIPING THE FACE OF JESUS
    (LEAVING AN IMAGE OF HIS FACE ON THE CLOTH);
7   JESUS FALLING UNDER THE WEIGHT OF THE CROSS
    (THE SECOND FALL);
8   JESUS ENCOUNTERING THE WOMEN OF JERUSALEM;
9   JESUS FALLING UNDER THE WEIGHT OF THE CROSS
    (THE THIRD FALL);
10 JESUS BEING STRIPPED OF HIS CLOTHES;
11 THE CRUCIFIXION;
12 THE DEATH;
13 THE DEPOSITION
    (JESUS' BODY BEING TAKEN DOWN FROM THE CROSS);
14 THE ENTOMBMENT.

✠

*Jesus meeting the Virgin Mary, the fourth Station
of the Cross, at the church of St Mary and All Saints,
Chesterfield, Derbyshire.*

Cruciform

Scroll Form

Triangular

Hexagonal

A HALO, or 'nimbus', appears in most church art around the head of a person of particular spiritual power. Halos are extremely useful from an artistic point of view, since they frame and highlight the head. Where an aura is portrayed around a whole figure it is known as an 'aureole' or 'mandorla'. The mandorla tends to be used for particular manifestations of God's power, such as THE TRANSFIGURATION, ASCENSION, or Second Coming.

Halos in art expanded over time, and then contracted again. In the earliest Christian art they were not used at all, and when they first appeared it was as see-through auras of light. By the Middle Ages, many halos had become vast golden cartwheels, but by the Renaissance they had shrunk again to discreet little hoops of light. After that it became acceptable again to dispense with them altogether.

In the Eastern Church, a halo signifies power rather than holiness. Images of Satan might be halo-ed to show his supernatural power, while persons in authority, such as kings or bishops, could be awarded halos as well. In the Western Church, the halo was reserved for people of sanctity. The cruciform halo is the most sacred. It appears around the head of Jesus (or in symbols for Jesus, such as the LAMB OF GOD), although it can also be applied to GOD THE FATHER and GOD THE HOLY SPIRIT. The Greek letters O WV, meaning 'I AM', or one of the Sacred Monograms, can appear within the cruciform halo. A triangular halo is sometimes added to images of God, to represent THE TRINITY. A six-pointed star, which is an ancient symbol of CREATION, can be used for the halo of God the Father. A square or scroll-shaped halo shows that the person portrayed as alive when the image was made. A hexagonal halo is sometimes applied to personifications of abstract ideas, such as the Virtues.

⁘

*Mary and the boy Jesus, Church of St Mary Virgin,
Tadcaster, North Yorkshire.*

ANIMALS, BIRDS, FISH & PLANTS

When decorating churches, many artists borrowed images from the natural world to represent Christian ideas or teaching. The world of nature was used as it appears in the Bible, for example from the way SHEEP are described there, or to illustrate aspects of Christian teaching, for example the transformation of a caterpillar into a BUTTERFLY illustrating resurrection. Particularly colourful analogies came from the medieval bestiaries. These

were books that both described known animals and recorded fantastic legends: of BEAR cubs born without shape, or LIONS covering up their tracks with their tails. On top of all of these, artists used analogies with mythical creatures. All these gave birth to a colourful menagerie in church art.

Just as artists used images of animals, birds, and FISH to illustrate Christian teaching, so too they used plants. Artists would portray plants in the way they are used in the Bible, or else would use characteristics of particular plants to make an analogy between them and parts of Christian teaching.

✛

Detail of a stone-carving of a mythical bird and (above) *a dragon's head on Strasbourg Cathedral, France.*

APE, BEAR & CAMEL

APE OR MONKEY

A MONKEY or APE was thought to be an animal with human desires but without human restraint. Thus it became a symbol of immoral self-indulgence, greed, cunning, and lust. A monkey in chains symbolizes the defeat, or at least civilized restraint, of these tendencies. It is often shown in exotic settings, or with exotic persons, such as THE MAGI.

BEAR

The BEAR is a symbol of evil power. The Prophet DANIEL had an apocalyptic vision of a bear with three tusks, one of four great beasts that symbolized four kingdoms that would arise and be defeated by God (Daniel 7; the bear has been taken to be the Kingdom of Persia). In one of the Bible's less attractive stories, a group of children shouted 'Clear off, baldy!' at the Prophet Elisha as he passed by their city. He cursed them, and two she-bears emerged from the woods, mauling forty-two of them (2 Kings 2:23–24). The scene is portrayed in the Chiesa della Ourita in Udine, Italy, an institution dedicated to the instruction of the (doubtless very respectful) young.

CAMEL

Since the CAMEL can go many days without drinking, it became a symbol of temperance, one of the seven virtues (see caption page 117). As an exotic creature, it is also associated in church art with exotic persons, such as THE MAGI or the Queen of Sheba. ST JOHN THE BAPTIST (page 209), a wild, ascetic holy man, dressed in camel's skin to preach repentance in the Judaean desert. Some artists took this reference literally, and he is shown draped with a one-piece camel skin, head and all.

✜

One of two carved monkeys on choir-stall ends at Winchester Cathedral, Hampshire. Monkeys are a symbol of greed, cunning and self-indulgence.

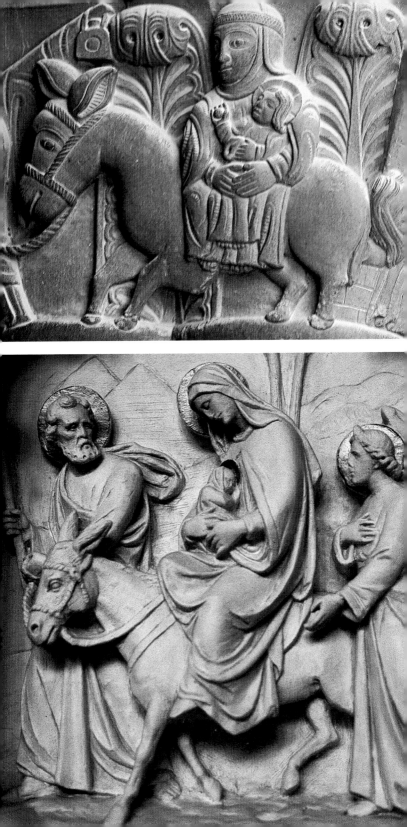

ASS & HORSE

ASS OR DONKEY

An ASS or DONKEY is a humble working animal, and so is a symbol of humility. They almost always appear in images of THE NATIVITY, and in many other stories, including THE SACRIFICE OF ISAAC. The backs of donkeys have a clear cross of dark hair, which according to legend appeared to commemorate Jesus' entry into Jerusalem on a donkey's back.

The most notorious ass in the Bible is that belonging to Balaam, from the Old Testament Book of Numbers. Balaam is an enigmatic figure, a blend of occult magician and legitimate prophet. On the one hand, a foreign king felt able to try to hire him to place a professional curse on the Israelites and weaken them in battle. On the other, he is shown consulting with God and obeying his commands. In the scene usually shown, Balaam had responded to the foreign king's summons and was travelling to see him on the back of his ass. Three times God placed an ANGEL in his path. Balaam could not see the angel, but the ass could and refused to take another step. When Balaam furiously beat the ass, God allowed it to speak and complain about his harsh treatment. The passage contains a rare biblical joke. The ass says, 'Am not I thine ass, upon which thou hast ridden ever since I was thine unto this day? Was I ever wont to do so unto thee?' Balaam's response is like an ass' cry: 'Nay!' (neigh) (Numbers 22:30, King James Version; when Balaam's response is translated as ' No!' the joke does not really work)

HORSES

The HORSE can also be a symbol of lust, after God's condemnation of the Israelites through the Prophet JEREMIAH: 'They are well-fed, lusty stallions, each neighing for another man's wife' (Jeremiah 5:8). ST GEORGE, as a warrior-saint, often rides a horse, while a man fallen from a horse may be ST PAUL on the road to Damascus.

⊹

Detail of a pillar capital depicting the Virgin Mary carrying Jesus while riding an ass and (bottom left) *a plaster relief depicting the Flight to Egypt at the church of St Mary, Bradford, Yorkshire.*

BULL, OXEN, PIG & STAG

BULL

When appearing with an EAGLE, a man, or a LION (most usually in a group of four), and especially when winged, the BULL is an emblem of ST LUKE.

OX

Especially when winged, the OX is a symbol of ST LUKE , and his Gospel. An ox is usually present at THE NATIVITY.

PIG

The PIG is a symbol of lust (*luxuria*), or greed (*avarita*), or sloth (*accidia*) – three of the seven deadly sins, the others being pride (*superbia*), anger (*ira*), envy (*invidia*) and sadness (*tristia*). It is also associated with the solitary ST ANTHONY OF EGYPT, born around 251 and regarded as the father of Christian monasticism. An order of hospitallers, founded in his name, kept pigs that were allowed to roam free in the town of La Motte in around 1100.

STAG OR DEER

A famous passage from the Psalms reads, 'As a stag longs for flowing streams, so my soul longs for you, O God!' (Psalm 42:1; modern translations replace the STAG with a DEER). A stag on its own is therefore a symbol of spiritual longing, while if it is drinking it is spiritual fulfilment. A stag with a cross between its antlers is a reference to the story either of St Hubert or St Eustace, both of whom were supposed to have been converted to Christianity when, while out hunting, they encountered a stag wearing a cross. It is not known if there was a 'historical' St Eustace (although he was supposed to be a Roman general, and can be distinguished from St Hubert by his dress), but he gained popularity from the story of his conversion and from his lurid martyrdom, roasted alive inside a hollow bronze BULL. More is known about St Hubert, who was Bishop of Maastricht in the eighth century. Both are patron saints of hunters.

✛

A pig or wild boar wood-carving, at St Mary, Mildenhall, Suffolk and (bottom right) *a carving of a stag on a stone corbel at the church of St Mary and St David, Kilpeck, Herefordshire.*

Lamb, Goat & Sheep

Lamb, Sheep and Shepherd

St John the Baptist was the first to call Jesus 'The Lamb of God'. He is often shown holding or standing next to a lamb whose head is usually surrounded by a cruciform halo, signifying Jesus. The image is reversed when Jesus is considered as the 'Good Shepherd', in which case the sheep are his people. The Bible is littered with sources for the image, which is an expression of the care that God has for humankind and the guidance he gives – but also the power he has over his flock. In the Old Testament, the images are of God as the gentle carer, particularly over the people of Israel ('The Lord is my shepherd, I shall not want', Psalm 23:1). Jesus is seen as fulfilling Old Testament prophecies of a shepherd who would come to guide humankind, and he described himself as the Good Shepherd. Jesus was portrayed by the early Christians as a young shepherd carrying a lamb on his shoulder.

The image is used in a more frightening way in images of The Last Judgement. Then, Jesus is the shepherd who will separate the sheep from the goats, with the sheep being the souls of the saved and the goats the souls of the damned. Images of the Final Judgement in this way are recognizable by this division. Other images of lambs, sheep, and rams are: on Abel's altar in the story of Cain and Abel; the ram that was caught in a bush in the story of Abraham and Isaac and with the shepherds at the Nativity. Twelve sheep or lambs together represent the Twelve Apostles, the twelve tribes of Israel, or all the faithful.

Ram

The ram is a symbol of Jesus. He is the leader of the herd; rams were thought to be able to defeat wolves (which represent the Devil); most importantly, in the story of Abraham and Isaac, the ram substituted as a sacrifice for Isaac was thought to prefigure Jesus, who was a substitute sacrifice for the whole of humankind.

✥

A stained-glass window depicting the Lamb of God, or Agnus Dei. *The lamb has Jesus' cruciform halo, and is bearing the flag of victory, indicating that Jesus is the sacrifice that has triumphed.*

Animals, Birds, Fish & Plants

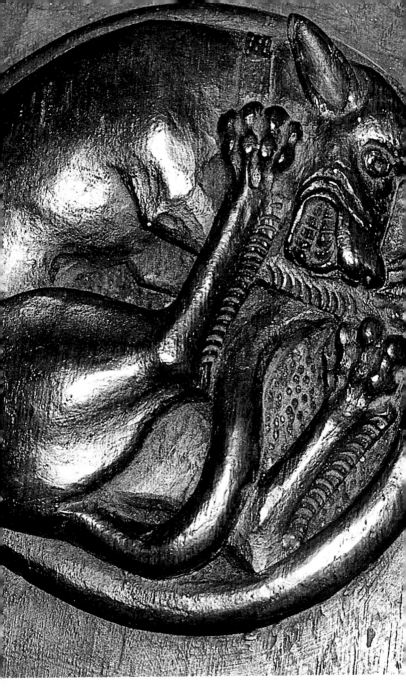

✣

A curled-up dog on a misericord (under a choir seat) at the church of St Edmund, Southwold, Suffolk and (right) a carved pew-end in the form of a rabbit.

Dog, Fox & Rabbit

Dog

Dogs are a common symbol of faithfulness, and regularly appear as such in both religious and secular art. In churches they are particularly common on tomb monuments, in honour of the person's fidelity. Dominican friars are sometimes symbolized by a black and white dog, in a pun on their name (*Domini canes*, dogs of the Lord) and their black and white robes.

In biblical times (and therefore in the Bible) dogs had a poor image. They are associated with snarling violence, or are seen in a contemptuous light as 'lowly' creatures. Jezebel suffered the ignominious fate of being eaten by dogs (2 Kings 9: 33–37), while in Jesus' parable of the rich man (Dives) and the poor man (Lazarus) 'even the dogs would come and lick his sores' (Luke 16: 21).

Fox

The fox is a traditional symbol of cunning, and may represent Satan. Samson destroyed the crops of the Philistines by tying burning torches to three hundred foxes' tails and releasing them into the wheat harvest (15 Judges 15:3-6).

Rabbit or Hare

The rabbit and the hare are common symbols of lust. This was partly through the rabbit's proverbial capacity to breed, and partly through a Latin pun: the Latin for rabbit is *cuniculus*; for vagina, it is *cunnus* (the root of a word in the modern vernacular).

A rabbit at the feet of the virgin mary symbolizes her victory over lust.

Lions & Unicorns

Lion

When appearing with a BULL, a man, or an EAGLE (usually in a group of four), and especially when winged, the LION is an emblem of ST MARK. Lions are also associated with DANIEL, SAMSON, who is often portrayed wearing the skin of the lion he killed, and St Jerome. Lions can symbolize strength and majesty, and so Jesus. They were meant to sleep with their eyes open, which made them a symbol of vigilance, just as Jesus is vigilant of the well-being of humankind. Some Christian writers pushed the analogy between Jesus and lions further, by reference to stories from the medieval bestiaries. Lion cubs were thought to be born dead, and come to life only when their father breathed life into them. More rarely, and depending on context, ravaging or devouring lions can symbolize the Devil, or evil, but when joined by other creatures, particularly a LAMB, the lion's ferocity is transformed into an image of the peace and tranquillity that is expected when God's kingdom is finally established. Powerful lions are defensive bulwarks in some Italian churches, where their statues support the porch columns.

Unicorn

The graceful UNICORN, a small white horselike beast with a single spiralling horn on its forehead, was adopted by Christians as a symbol of God's incarnation in Jesus, and Jesus' sinless life. In Roman mythology the unicorn was powerful, wild, and impossible to catch by force. But it loved purity and could be tamed by a virgin, in whose lap it would lay its head and sleep. This combination of purity and strength made this a popular analogy, particularly as all-powerful God came to the womb of THE VIRGIN MARY, just as the untameable unicorn would come to virgins. In addition, the horn of the unicorn was believed to be an antidote to poison (for which purpose narwhal horns used to be sold as unicorn horns). Correspondingly, Jesus was an antidote to sin.

✣

*Detail from a stained-glass window of
a lion with human bones and skull, Ely Cathedral,
Cambridgeshire.*

BASILISK & PHOENIX

BASILISK

The BASILISK, also known as the cockatrice, was half SERPENT and half COCKEREL. It could be created through hatching a hen's egg under a SNAKE or a toad. The basilisk was the king of serpents, and is portrayed with a high cockerel's comb, a serpent's tail, and chicken's wings. They were deadly monsters, killing instantly with their breath or just with a look. Even if speared, the basilisk's deadly poison would shoot through the spear to kill the holder and any HORSE he might be riding on. All of this made the basilisk an obvious symbol for the Devil. This connection was made explicit in one translation of Psalm 91:13: 'Thou shalt tread upon the adder and the basilisk and trample underfoot the lion, and the dragon'.

St Augustine interpreted the adder, the basilisk, the LION, and the DRAGON as representing aspects of the Devil: the adder is cunning; the lion is open rage; the dragon is hidden plotting; the basilisk is the king of serpents, as the Devil is the king of wicked spirits. In mythology, the basilisk's only natural enemy was the weasel, which was impervious to its deadliness. The weasel has never been taken up as a symbol in Christian art, but is a prime candidate.

PHOENIX

The PHOENIX resembles an EAGLE with brilliantly colourful plumage (often scarlet and gold), and is portrayed rising from a raging fire. The story of the phoenix was told, with variations, from Ancient Egypt and Greece through to Asia and China. There was only ever one phoenix at any one time, and it lived for up to a thousand years. When the time came for it to die, it would make itself a nest of spices, and sing a song so beautiful that the sun god would stop to listen. Sparks from the sun would set the nest alight, consuming the old phoenix. A rejuvenated phoenix would then rise up from the flames. The uniqueness and splendour of the phoenix, its dying and rising again, and its symbolism of hope in the face of death, caused it to be adopted as a symbol for Jesus and his RESURRECTION, and the Christian's triumph over death. It also came to be a symbol of the undying and eternal City of Rome.

SNAKES AND SERPENTS

SNAKES usually symbolize the Devil, or sin. In the GARDEN OF EDEN, it was a SERPENT that persuaded the first-created woman, Eve, to eat the forbidden fruit of the Tree of the Knowledge of Good and Evil, so allowing sin to enter and damage what had been until then a perfect world. When he discovered what the snake had done, God pronounced a curse on it: 'Cursed are you above all the livestock and all the wild animals! You will crawl on your belly and you will eat dust all the days of your life. And I will put enmity between you and the woman, and between your offspring and hers; he will crush your head, and you will strike his heel' (Genesis 3:14–15).

Snakes appearing grasped in a hand or squashed underfoot symbolize Jesus' (or the Christian's) triumph over sin. A snake at the foot of the cross in a CRUCIFIXION scene shows that sin has been defeated

In contrast, when mounted on a staff, a snake is a symbol of Jesus. The image is derived from the story of the bronze serpent in EXODUS, when the Israelites were saved from a plague of snakes by a bronze serpent that MOSES had raised on a pole. Jesus made an explicit connection between the bronze serpent and his crucifixion ('Just as Moses lifted up the snake in the desert, so the Son of Man must be lifted up'; John 3:14). From the same story, the symbol of a snake entwined with a pole is a symbol of healing.

When hovering over a cup or chalice, a snake is associated with ST JOHN. The snake represents the poison in the chalice that John was challenged to drink as proof of his authority from God.

Finally, snakes can be used as an emblem of God's authority. God transformed Moses' staff into a snake and back into a staff, as a proof to the Israelites (and later to Pharaoh) that God had appeared to him and to Aaron (Exodus 4 & 7). When Pharaoh's sorcerers performed the same feat, the snake from Moses' staff swallowed up the snakes from the sorcerers' staffs.

✣

A cross crushes the head of a coiled serpent symbolising triumph over sin.

GRIFFIN & DRAGON

GRIFFIN (OR GRYPHON)

The GRIFFIN was a monster with the head and wings of an EAGLE, and the body and legs of a LION. They were good at gold: different legends had them knowing instinctively where gold could be found, making their nests out of gold, or guarding gold mines.

The griffin was used as a symbol for Jesus, for a number of reasons. The two elements of the griffin were like the human (lion on the earth) and divine (eagle in the sky) aspects of Jesus' nature; the lion and the eagle were respectively kings of the animals and of the birds; and it combined a lion's strength with an eagle's vigilance. It remained, though, a tricky image, suggesting at the same time ferocity, knowledge (particularly as regards money), and usury.

DRAGON

St Michael slaying Satan, as dragon

DRAGONS, reptilian winged monsters, exist in the mythology of almost all cultures. In the Bible, the dragon symbolizes Satan, as it was the shape taken by him in the Book of Revelation. The Book of Revelation describes a war in heaven, between the angels of God, led by the ARCHANGEL MICHAEL, and Satan and his rebel angels. The dragon ('an enormous red dragon with seven heads and ten horns and seven crowns on his heads') and the rebel angels are hurled to earth, whereupon they go to make war with Jesus' followers (Revelation 12 & 13). Where a dragon is portrayed being defeated by an angel – often run through with a spear and trampled underfoot – it is a depiction of Satan's defeat by Michael.

A dragon is also depicted in pictures of ST GEORGE. These can be distinguished from depictions of St Michael because St Michael is winged, whereas St George is a knight on horseback, usually with his badge of a red cross on a white background on his shield or breastplate.

❖

St George – patron saint of England – vanquishing the dragon, depicted in a stained-glass window at the church of St Mary, Happisburgh, Norfolk.

To the ... of God

Leviathan & Salamander

LEVIATHAN

LEVIATHAN is a mythical beast which appears in the Old Testament, sometimes portrayed as a sea-serpent, sometimes as a fish, but important because of its great size. It is most often used as a metaphor to show the power of God, who can defeat this mighty animal (Psalm 74:14, Isaiah 27:1).

Leviathan is associated with (or taken to be the same as) Satan, and is connected with hell. Representation of the entrance to hell as a vast, fishy jaw come from the vivid description of Leviathan in Job 41: 'From its mouth go flaming torches; sparks of fire leap out. Out of its nostrils comes smoke, as from a boiling pot and burning rushes.'

SALAMANDER

In ancient mythology, SALAMANDERS were fireproof, and could even extinguish fire. They therefore came to symbolize the virtue of the righteous man, and his power to resist the fiery temptation of sin.

Scorpion & Frog

SCORPION

The sudden sting of the SCORPION gave it a reputation for evil, and is in particular associated with JUDAS ISCARIOT.

FROG

FROGS are a relatively rare symbol, of punishment and of demonic powers. One of the PLAGUES OF EGYPT was of frogs sent by God as a punishment (Exodus 8). Frogs appear in the Book of Revelation as the appearance adopted by certain evil spirits (Revelation 16:13) and demonic spirits are often portrayed in Christian art as being frog-like.

✣

A sea serpent on a pew-end in the church of All Saints, Hollesley, Suffolk. and (bottom left) *a carved frog on a pew-end at the church of St Andrew, Hingham, Norfolk.*

WHALES & FISH

WHALES

A WHALE is most often associated with JONAH, and whales have an old association with devilry. Sailors believed that whales would pretend to be islands. When a ship anchored on them, they would plunge into the depths, dragging the ship with them. Jonah's three days in the belly of the whale were thought to prefigure Jesus' three days in hell.

FISH

The FISH is a symbol for Jesus, while three fishes interwoven is a fairly common symbol of THE TRINITY. The fish also later became a  symbol for THE EUCHARIST, and if pictured near a chalice represents the bread, the body of Jesus.

Fishes feature most prominently in two New Testament stories. Jesus' blessed five loaves and two fishes and was miraculously able to feed a crowd of five thousand. At the start of his ministry Jesus promised to two of his fishermen disciples, the brothers ST PETER and ST ANDREW, that if they left their nets and followed him then he would make them 'fishers of men'. After Jesus' resurrection the disciples were fishing in the early morning on the Sea of Galilee, but had caught nothing. Jesus appeared and told them to cast their net on the other side, when it was filled so full that they could not raise it and had to drag it back to shore (John 21: 4 – 14). The story of the heavy net has been taken as a metaphor for the number of souls that the disciples were to save, with God's guidance, and fishes are sometimes used as a symbol of people's souls.

Like the image of the shepherd and the SHEEP, the image of the fish has a darker side, as a warning about THE LAST JUDGEMENT of God. Jesus said that the kingdom of heaven is like a net that was let down into the lake and caught all kinds of fish.

 When it was full, the fishermen pulled it up on the shore. Then they sat down and collected the good fish in baskets, but threw the bad away (Matthew 13:47–48).

✣

The Prophet Jonah is spewed onto dry land by the great fish (Jonah 2:10), and (below) a carving on a Norman font depicting St John the Baptist baptizing Jesus – note the four fish.

Birds, Bees & Insects

Birds

Birds, as inhabitants of the air and the earth, were an ancient Egyptian symbol of the soul, a symbol that was adopted by the early Christians. Charming legends grew up around some species. During THE CRUCIFIXION, the robin was said to have fluttered around Jesus, desperately trying to staunch the flow of blood from his wounds with its own body. In honour of this, it has ever since been marked with a blood-red breast. The sparrow, on the other hand, hopped around the foot of the cross, jeering at Jesus. It was cursed to move forever on the earth in sharp, hopping jumps.

Bee or Beehive

The BEE or BEEHIVE is a symbol of St Ambrose, who spoke with honeyed words and on whose mouth a swarm of bees was meant to have settled without harming him. The beehive can also be a symbol of the organized and industrious Church (with Christians as the bees), an analogy used by St Ambrose himself. See also SAMSON (page 284)

Flies

Images of FLIES need to be treated with care. The fly has been used as a symbol of illness, evil, and sin (Beelzebub, the name of a powerful demon, or Satan himself, is a Hebrew word that translates as 'Lord of the Flies'). However, images of flies were also thought to have a practical purpose. It was believed that a fly painted onto a sacred object repelled the real insects, and prevented them from profaning the images with their touch.

Butterflies

Butterflies can symbolize RESURRECTION, transformation, and new life, because they have cast off their previous existence as creeping caterpillars. They sometimes appear in images of Jesus as a child.

✣

Carved pew-end of a bee landing
on a flower at the church of St Andrew, Hingham, Norfolk.

DOVE & GOLDFINCH

DOVE

In Christian art, a dove is most commonly a symbol of God the Holy Spirit, and appears in images of the annunciation, the baptism of jesus, and of the trinity. A dove is also prominent in the story of noah. In the Old Testament a pair of doves (or pigeons) was declared an appropriate sacrifice for purification after the birth of a child (Leviticus 5:7), and joseph took a pair of pigeons as a sacrifice when Jesus was presented at the Temple (Luke 2:22–24). As sacrificial objects, doves or pigeons also appear in scenes of the expulsion of the moneychangers, since the sellers of doves for sacrifice was one of the groups that Jesus drove out of the Temple precincts. Finally, doves are often used to represent the human soul. When there are twelve of them, they represent the twelve apostles, the twelve tribes of Israel, or all humankind

GOLDFINCH

For all of their vivid beauty and delicacy, GOLDFINCHES were thought to live on a diet of THISTLES and spiny plants, which symbolize the troubles of the world, or Jesus' CROWN OF THORNS. They sometimes appear in images of Jesus as a child, when they contrast his youthful innocence with the suffering he would endure as an adult. In a direct connection between the goldfinch and THE PASSION, a goldfinch was said to have tried to pull a thorn, from the crown of thorns, from Jesus' forehead. In the process it was splashed with a drop of Jesus' blood, which became the permanent red mark on its head.

✣

A stained glass panel and (below) *a stone-carving of the dove returning to Noah's Ark over the flooded land, carrying an olive branch in its beak.*

EAGLE, OWL & RAVEN

EAGLE

As an ancient familiar of Jupiter, ruler of the gods, and a symbol of Rome, the EAGLE has had a long association with power and the divine. It is most often used as a symbol of ST JOHN the Evangelist and of his Gospel. Church LECTERNS, which support the Bible for readings, are very often in the shape of an eagle with spread wings, because the eagle was a symbol of divine inspiration. Medieval bestiaries said that the eagle renewed its plumage each year by flying near the sun and then plunging into water. Like the PHOENIX, the eagle therefore came to be used as a symbol of THE RESURRECTION, and so of Jesus.

OWL

An OWL was the traditional familiar of the Greek goddess of wisdom, Athene This association caused it in turn to become an attribute of St Jerome, who was thought a fountain of wisdom. The owl is often also a symbol of the night, darkness, and evil. It is sometimes present at THE CRUCIFIXION, where it symbolizes the darkness into which Jesus gives light.

RAVEN

Although in art and literature RAVENS tend to be birds of ill-omen, in the Bible they enjoy a happier reputation. A raven was the first bird that NOAH sent from the Ark to see if the floodwaters had receded, before sending out the more famous DOVE. In Jewish legend, the raven was white as snow when Noah sent it out, and only turned black when it failed to return. Ravens are also honoured in the Bible as having been sent by God with food for the Prophet Elijah and a number of later stories show ravens feeding hermit saints in the desert. Jesus also used ravens positively in one of his most famous sayings: 'Consider the ravens: They do not sow or reap, they have no storeroom or barn; yet God feeds them. And how much more valuable you are than birds!' (Luke 12:24).

❖

Wood-carving of an eagle, portal at the basilica of St Francis, Assisi, Italy. The eagle is a symbol of divine inspiration, and is most frequently associated with St John the Evangelist.

PEACOCK & PELICAN

PEACOCK

Medieval bestiaries claimed the PEACOCK did not decay after it died, and so it became a symbol of immortality and THE RESURRECTION. The peacock is particularly closely associated with THE VIRGIN MARY: firstly, the bird was the familiar of Juno, Roman queen of the gods, and so was already associated with the Queen of Heaven; secondly, Mary's body was thought to have been assumed, undecayed like the peacock's, into heaven.

PELICAN

The PELICAN was said to peck at its breast in order to feed its young with its own blood, or to revive them by sprinkling its blood. This selfless giving of its blood to feed, nurture, and save its offspring, was seen as a direct analogy with Jesus' sacrifice.

COCKEREL, CRANE & STORK

COCKEREL

The COCK, crying out at dawn, is a symbol of vigilance against the wiles of the Devil. It is also an attribute of ST PETER because of the cockcrow after his three denials of Christ.

CRANE

The CRANE is a symbol of vigilance. Cranes were said to gather in a circle to sleep, while one of their number stayed on watch. The watcher's system for keeping awake was to stand on one foot. If it dozed, the raised foot would fall, and it would wake.

STORK

In the bestiaries the STORK fed its parents in their old age, and so it became a symbol of filial duty. As a herald of spring, it also became a symbol of the announcement of Jesus' birth at THE ANNUNCIATION.

✣

A stained-glass window depicting the 'Pelican in Her Piety',
feeding her young with her own blood.
This was seen as an analogy with Jesus' sacrifice.

ACACIA BUSH

Traditionally, THE BURNING BUSH was an ACACIA. When an acacia bush is topped with flames, it represents this event . The bush was said to be on fire but not destroyed and therefore acacia bushes also represent the immortality of the soul.

JESSE TREE

The Book of Isaiah contains a prophecy regarding the Messiah: 'A shoot will come up from the stump of Jesse; from his roots a branch will bear fruit. The Spirit of the Lord will rest on him – the Spirit of wisdom and of understanding, the Spirit of counsel and of power, the Spirit of knowledge and of the fear of the Lord – and he will delight in the fear of the Lord.'

Jesse was the father of KING DAVID. The prophecy was taken in Christian teaching to be of Jesus, because he was a direct descendant of Jesse. This is the origin of the 'JESSE TREE'. The tree is often pictured springing up from a sleeping figure, which may be Jesse, ABRAHAM, or ADAM (if it is Adam, the tree may be growing out of his chest, in a reference to the creation of EVE from Adam's rib; if it is Jesse, the tree may be growing out of the poor man's loins). An alternative variety of Jesse tree is hung with the symbols of the story of God's revelation to humanity, from creation to Jesus' resurrection, for example, the hanging symbols might include an apple (Adam and Eve), rainbow (NOAH), BURNING BUSH (MOSES), harp (DAVID), LILY (MARY), and FISH (Jesus).

ASPEN

The delicate leaves of the ASPEN tree quiver at the slightest breeze, which has given rise to delightful legends. One is that it was aspen wood that was used for the cross of THE CRUCIFIXION. When the aspen realized the terrible purpose to which it was to be put, it started trembling and has never stopped. Another is that alone among the trees it refused to bow to Jesus as he hung on the cross and so was cursed to tremble for eternity

ALMOND & APPLE

ALMOND

ALMONDS are a symbol of divine favour and, because of their early flowering, prophecy. They are also associated with THE VIRGIN MARY, because of their symbolism of divine favour, the pure white of their blossom, and the womblike shape of the almond's nut. The Angel GABRIEL's first words to Mary, when announcing that she was chosen to be the mother of the Son of God, were 'Greetings, you who are highly favoured! The Lord is with you' (Luke 1:27).

APPLE

God told ADAM AND EVE that they could eat from any tree in the Garden of Eden, except the Tree of the Knowledge of Good and Evil. A SERPENT tempted Eve, who in turn tempted Adam, to eat this forbidden fruit, in humankind's first act of disobedience to God.

The Bible does not say what kind of fruit grew on the Tree of the Knowledge of Good and Evil, but the most common tradition is that it was an APPLE, though a strong case is also made for the fig, since it was fig leaves that Adam and Eve clothed themselves in. An alternative tradition even names the orange as the offending fruit.

The Latin word for apple, *malum*, is also an adjective meaning 'evil'. When held by Adam, an apple symbolizes sin. When held by Jesus or THE VIRGIN MARY, it symbolizes salvation and triumph over sin. The idea of the apple in Jesus' hand being sweet after the bitterness of Adam's apple was thought to be predicted by the Song of Solomon: 'Like an apple tree among the trees of the forest is my lover among the young men. I delight to sit in his shade and his fruit is sweet to my taste' (2:3).

When three apples are shown, in a basket alone or with roses or other fruit, it is a symbol of St Dorothy (d. *circa* 304). On the way to her execution for refusing to renounce her Christian beliefs, Dorothy was jeered at by a young lawyer named Theophilus, who challenged her to send him fruit and flowers from paradise. An ANGEL later brought Theophilus a basket containing three apples and three ROSES. He quickly converted to Christianity.

ANIMALS, BIRDS, FISH & PLANTS

Vine & Grapes, Olive & Pomegranate

Vine and grapes

As an important crop in ancient Palestine, the VINE is an Old Testament symbol of abundance. Their association with the wine of THE EUCHARIST gives them a vital symbolic purpose. When seen with WHEAT, GRAPES symbolize the wine used in the Eucharist. In the New Testament, the vine symbolizes Jesus (John 15:5). A vineyard can also symbolize the Church.

Olive branch and leaf

The OLIVE BRANCH is a universal symbol of peace and prosperity, visually when clasped in the beak of a DOVE, or verbally when we talk of the olive branch of peace. The dove sent out by NOAH returned with an OLIVE LEAF in its beak to show that the waters had receded. One of the seven foods that God promised to the Israelites in the Promised Land (the others being WHEAT, barley, VINES, fig trees, POMEGRANATES, and honey, Deuteronomy 8:7) olives appear repeatedly in the Bible when representing wealth, or the destruction of wealth.

Pomegranate

Fruits bursting with seeds, POMEGRANATES are symbols of fertility and bounty. A single pomegranate may also symbolize the Church, as it has many segments and seeds within the one fruit. In classical mythology, Persephone (in Roman mythology, Proserpina) was the daughter of Zeus (Jove), the king of the gods, and Demeter (Ceres), the goddess of the harvest. She was so beautiful that Hades (Pluto), god of the underworld, took her to be his queen. When Demeter discovered this, she went to reclaim her. But Persephone had eaten four pomegranate seeds while in the underworld, which gave Hades a claim on her. She was therefore to live in the underworld for one month each year for each seed she had eaten, during which time winter would reign.

✜

Neo-Gothic decoration by Pugin at the church of St Giles, Cheadle, Staffordshire.

BRAMBLE, THORN & ROSE

BRAMBLE

An alternative tradition names the BRAMBLE, rather than the ACACIA, as the plant within THE BURNING BUSH.

With THORNS and THISTLES, brambles may symbolize earthly hardship, or desolation: 'Thorns will overrun her citadels, nettles and brambles her strongholds. She will become a haunt for jackals, a home for owls' (Isaiah 34:13).

THORN

After he was condemned to death, Roman soldiers placed a CROWN OF THORNS on Jesus' head, in mockery of his claim to be the King of Jews. The crown of thorns was a parody of the crown of ROSES that the Roman Emperor wore at festivals. The crown is traditionally portrayed as a circular woven ring, because the soldiers are recorded as having twisted thorns into a crown. When it is placed with other instruments of Jesus' suffering such as the CROSS, nails, or whip, the crown of thorns is also a symbol of Good Friday.

A flowering thorn bush may represent the Glastonbury thorn, which in England is a symbol of THE NATIVITY. The reference is to an ancient English tradition. Joseph of Arimathea was said to have returned to England after Jesus' resurrection to spread the Gospel. Tired from his journey, he rested on Glastonbury Hill and stuck his staff in the ground. When he awoke, the staff had taken root and blossomed. It blossomed every year around Christmas time, and so an association with Christmas and the Nativity arose. There is still a thorn bush at Glastonbury Abbey which, it is claimed, is descended from that planted by Joseph of Arimathea.

With THISTLES and BRAMBLES, thorns can be a symbol of the hardship of life, derived from the reference in Genesis. Jesus in his parable of the sower took the image further. He used the thistle to symbolize life's worries, riches, and pleasures, which can choke the word of God. Jesus told the story of a farmer

✧

Intricate metalwork design of flowers, foliage and fruit.

who went out to sow his seed. Some of the seed fell on hard ground where it was eaten by the birds; some on rock, where it died for no moisture; some fell among thorns, which grew up and choked it; some fell on fertile ground, where it yielded a huge crop. Jesus explained the parable to his disciples. The seed was the word of God. Some people would hear the word of God, and then the Devil (the birds) would come and take away the word from their hearts; some are like the rock, who receive the word with joy, but have no root and fall away; the seed that fell among thorns stands for those who hear, but are ultimately choked by life's worries, riches, and pleasures, and they do not mature; the seed on good soil stands for those who hear the word and by persevering produce a crop (Luke 8).

Rose

The ROSE symbolizes purity, and THE VIRGIN MARY. St Ambrose related a legend of the rose. Before the Fall, he said, the rose had no thorns. When it developed them after the Fall, it was as a poignant reminder of the disaster that had taken place: the beauty and scent of the rose was to remind humankind

The Rose

of the paradise that it had lost, while the thorns were a reminder of the barrier that had been created and the suffering humankind had now to endure. Roses therefore show heavenly joy, when they are worn by angels or persons who are in heaven. Derived from the same legend, Mary is sometimes called the 'rose without thorns', because she was thought to have been without sin. If you look carefully at images of the Virgin Mary that also show roses growing, you should see that the stems are smooth. Mary also took the rose as an attribute since it was the flower of Venus, Roman goddess of love, and because of a verse from the Song of Solomon that was thought to relate to her: 'I am a rose of Sharon, the lily of the valleys' (2:1).

The blood-red rose is a symbol of martyrdom, the white a symbol of purity and perfect beauty.

✤

A ceiling boss in the form of a rose.

CLOVER, WHEAT & THISTLE

CLOVER

With its three leaves in a single plant, CLOVER is a symbol of THE TRINITY.

WHEAT

WHEAT, whether in single stalks or bound in a sheaf, has a number of interlocking meanings. It is a symbol of the bread used in THE EUCHARIST, and this will be its meaning when it is placed together with GRAPES, which symbolize the wine of the Eucharist. Wheat is a symbol of the word of God, from the parable of the sower. It is also a regular biblical emblem of God's bountifulness. In a sheaf it is therefore a symbol of the Harvest Festival and of thanksgiving.

Wheat was also used to show Jesus' human nature, and to convey a message of hope. Jesus predicted his death, and the hope of his RESURRECTION, through an analogy with wheat dying: 'The hour has come for the Son of Man to be glorified. I tell you the truth, unless a kernel of wheat falls to the ground and dies, it remains only a single seed. But if it dies, it produces many seeds' (John 12:24). It can also be incorporated into images of THE LAST JUDGEMENT, as a symbol of the good soul – '[God's] winnowing fork is in his hand to clear his threshing floor and to gather the wheat into his barn, but he will burn up the chaff with unquenchable fire' (Matthew 3:12; Luke 3:17).

THISTLE

THISTLES are a symbol for earthly hardship and sin. The source of the image is God's curse on ADAM, when he had broken God's prohibition from eating from the Tree of the Knowledge of Good and Evil: 'Cursed is the ground because of you; through painful toil you will eat of it all the days of your life. It will produce THORNS and thistles for you, and you will eat the plants of the field'. The thistle is also used in the Old Testament as a symbol of earthly desolation (Hosea 8).

ANIMALS, BIRDS, FISH & PLANTS

Anemone & Narcissus

Anemone

With its three large outer petals, the ANEMONE is a symbol of THE TRINITY. The spots of red colour on the petals of some anemones were thought to represent drops of Jesus' blood at THE CRUCIFIXION. Anemones are sometimes shown growing at the foot of the cross in images of the scene, since according to legend they sprang up over Golgotha that evening. The image is probably borrowed from classical mythology, since the beautiful Adonis was said to have died on a bed of anemones, which were stained red with his blood.

Narcissus

In Christian imagery, the NARCISSUS symbolizes divine love. The symbol derives from an ancient Greek myth, of a beautiful young man called Narcissus, who spent so long admiring his own reflection in a pool of water that he died there, and the flower that is now named after him sprang up on the spot. In a Christian context, the image has been turned around, from a symbol of self-love into a symbol of the triumph of divine love.

Christmas Rose & Columbine

Christmas rose

Unsurprisingly, THE CHRISTMAS ROSE is a symbol of Christmas, or THE NATIVITY.

Columbine

COLUMBINE is a symbol of THE HOLY SPIRIT, through its supposed resemblance to a DOVE. The plant's name comes from the Latin for dove, *columba*, though it was also known as *herba leonis*, from a belief that it was the favourite herb of the LION.

✢

IRIS

IRISES are also known as sword lilies. As such, they are occasionally, although rarely, used as a symbol of THE VIRGIN MARY.

LILY

In modern times, the LILY has come to be associated with death, but in a church it is always associated in some way with THE VIRGIN MARY. Images of Mary often have her holding a lily, or one might stand in a vase beside her. Perhaps because of their close association with the Virgin Mary, lilies are also associated with the ARCHANGEL GABRIEL and ST JOSEPH.

The Lily

The arum lily is sometimes known as Gethsemane and was supposed to have been sprinkled with Jesus' blood as it grew at the foot of the CROSS.

In the Song of Solomon, the Bible's great love poem, the lily is also a symbol of great beauty: 'Like a lily among thorns is my darling among the maidens' (Song of Solomon 2:22). The Song of Solomon was interpreted by some Christian writers as representing Jesus' love for his Church, and the lily is associated with the beauty of the Church.

VIOLET

VIOLETS are a symbol of humility, because they grow low and have small flowers. Violets are particularly associated with THE VIRGIN MARY, through her humility in accepting the motherhood of God, and with Christ, in accepting humanity.

✣

Mary with Jesus and lilies; Presbytery, Grange Road, Easton.
In churches, the lily is
always associated with the Virgin Mary.

Holly, Ivy & Laurel

Holly

The HOLLY is a symbol of Jesus' suffering, because according to one legend it provided the wood for the cross of THE CRUCIFIXION. The trees of the forest splintered into fragments at the touch of the woodsman's axe, rather than be used to make the cross; only the holly did not. Its symbolism is explored exhaustively in the ancient hymn, 'The Holly and the Ivy', where the spines represent THE CROWN OF THORNS, the white flowers purity and the birth of Jesus, the red berries drops of blood, and the bitter bark THE PASSION.

> The holly and the ivy
> When they are both full grown
> Of all the trees that are in the wood
> The holly bears the crown …

Ivy

Ivy is such a useful decorative feature – it can be found wound around pillars, framing altars, or in any manner of positions – that it is dangerous to over-emphasize its symbolic purpose. However, as an evergreen it is a symbol of immortality; and as it grows by clinging to supports, it is a symbol of fidelity.

Laurel

LAUREL leaves woven into a crown are a pre-Christian symbol of victory, awarded to winners of ancient games and held above the triumphant victors of battles. They were therefore adopted as a symbol of Christian victory: Jesus' (and so the Christian's) victory over death, sin, and the world. PAUL refers to the laurel obliquely in his Letter to the Corinthians, when he compares the prize to be awarded to followers of Jesus with the prize awarded to competitors in games (1 Corinthians 9:24–27).

As laurel leaves that have been cut do not wilt or change their colour, they are, like HOLLY and IVY, symbolic of eternity and everlasting life. Laurel is also associated with chastity, since the laurel was the plant of the Vestal Virgins in Rome.

Bulrush, Palm Leaf & Oak

Bulrush

Bulrushes show God's power to nurture, sustain, and save. The symbol is taken from the Book of Job. God commented to Satan that Job was a truly good man. Satan responded that Job would curse God if he allowed Satan to afflict him. God allowed Satan to test Job in this way, and Job was tormented with boils. While Job was suffering, his splendidly named companion Bildad the Shuhite tried to comfort him: 'Can papyrus grow tall where there is no marsh? Can bulrushes thrive without water? While still growing and uncut, they wither more quickly than grass. Such is the destiny of all who forget God; so perishes the hope of the godless' (Job 8:11–13).

Palm leaf

The PALM LEAF has been associated with victory since pre-Christian times. It was therefore a logical step for it to become a symbol of Jesus' victory over death, and of the Christian's victory over sin, the world, and the Devil. Jesus made his triumphant ENTRY INTO JERUSALEM with a palm in his hand and the road was spread with palm branches cut from the fields.
Commonly used as a symbol is of martyrdom, it is often referred to in Christian literature as the martyr's palm. The martyr's palm held or near to a figure will indicate that that person was a martyr.

Oak

The sturdy OAK is a symbol of strength, durability, faith, and endurance. The symbol can also be reversed into one of pride, in God laying low the apparently strong: 'The Lord Almighty has a day in store for all the proud and lofty … for all the cedars of Lebanon, tall and lofty, and all the oaks of Bashan … the arrogance of man will be brought low and the pride of men humbled' (Isaiah 2; Amos 2:9).

The oak also appears in the dramatic Old Testament story of KING DAVID and his rebellious son Absalom (2 Samuel 18). The story gives rise to the word 'Absalomism' – a son's rebellion against his father.

NUMBERS & SHAPES, LETTERS, WORDS & COLOURS

NUMBERS and SHAPES can be significant when incorporated into images, for example the triangle as a symbol of THE TRINITY, or twelve sheep being a reference to the disciples. They can also be important in church furniture, for example in octagonal FONTS and PULPITS, and even in the church fabric. It is undoubtedly true that the number of windows appearing in a facade will be dictated by the demands of the building, but a group of, say, three can also be a reference to the Trinity. It is therefore worth considering separately the symbolism of numbers and shapes.

In traditional churches the year is colour-coded. The colour of the fabric used on the altar and the vestments of the priest, for example, will change according to the season. These are the 'liturgical colours', and the standard colours are green, purple, white, and red. Colours can also have symbolic meanings, for example in the colour of clothes given to a particular saint.

Look out for LETTERS and WORDS, carved or painted, in churches. Some of these words will be straightforward translations of key passages from the Bible. Letters, such as IHC, IHS, and the CHI RHO (which, since they all indicate Jesus in some way, are known together as the Sacred Monograms), have taken on a symbolic life of their own.

✣

The Greek letters alpha (top) and omega (bottom) on the altar frontal at the church of St Alkelda, Giggleswick, North Yorkshire.

NUMBERS & SHAPES

The circle was considered by the ancient Greeks to be the perfect shape – eternal, without beginning or end, a perfectly balanced whole. A single circle is therefore a symbol of the divine, or eternity, while the number one expresses the unity of God.

The number two is used in reference to the human and divine natures of Jesus, or to the Old and the New Testaments. The number three is extensively used as a symbol of THE TRINITY, particularly in association with a triangle. The triangle in this meaning is always equilateral, in order to represent the equality of the three persons of the Trinity. It can also represent the three days that Jesus spent in the tomb, before THE RESURRECTION.

The number four can represent THE FOUR EVANGELISTS. It may also be the number of rivers that the book of Genesis said flowed from Eden (the Pishon, the Gihon, the Tigris, and the Euphrates; Genesis 2:10–14). It is also a warning reminder of the four horsemen of the apocalypse, described in the sixth chapter of the Book of Revelation, who were unleashed with authority over a quarter of the earth, and have been interpreted as representing conquest (white horse, rider crowned and carrying a bow), war (red horse, rider carries a sword), famine (black horse, rider with scales), and death (green horse, rider usually skeletal). The form of a square or cube is a symbol for the earth. It is a solid, unmoving form, just as the earth is (or rather, as it was perceived to be). A square HALO was used on images of holy people who were still alive at the time when the image was made. It forms a contrast with the 'divine' shape of the circle.

Five symbolizes the five wounds that Jesus suffered in THE CRUCIFIXION (the four nails in his hands and feet, and the spear in his side).

Seven is significant as a powerful mystical number that appears repeatedly through the Bible, and is associated with perfection. A few examples of this are: God resting on the seventh day after completing CREATION; JACOB bowing seven times before his brother Esau, as a sign of perfect submission (Genesis 34:2–4); God ordering that the lampstand for THE TABERNACLE during THE EXODUS should have seven branches

(Exodus 25:37); and the seven angels blowing their trumpets in the apocalypse (Revelation 8–11).

The number eight, through the octagon, is a symbol of Jesus, unifying God and earth. An octagon is 'halfway' between a circle (God) and a square (earth). Just as Jesus was the incarnation of God on Earth, so the octagon mediates between these two. This idea of heaven and earth coming into contact lies behind the octagonal shapes of some FONTS and PULPITS. At the baptism of a person, heaven and earth touch, while during a sermon the preacher is communicating the word of God.

Nine is the number of the angels, since there are nine choirs of them. Ten is the number of THE TEN COMMANDMENTS.

The number twelve in a church will refer to the twelve disciples, which in turn refers to the twelve tribes of Israel. Since in both instances it is the number of a group of people dedicated to God, it is sometimes used to represent the whole church. The number thirteen, on the other hand, is ominous, and indicates betrayal, since it was the number of people present around the table at THE LAST SUPPER (twelve disciples, plus Jesus).

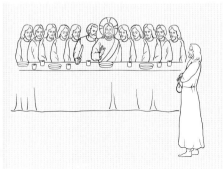

In images of the Last Supper, Judas is often pictured standing apart from Jesus and the other Disciples; he is also seen to be holding a purse, alluding to the thirty pieces of silver that he received in return for betraying Jesus.

Finally, although the number forty does not much come into play in church design or imagery, it is important in a number of Bible stories, associated with periods of trial or repentance (the word 'quarantine' comes from the Latin for forty, this being the number of days that penitents had to spend in isolation). Rather than denoting a precise sum, it can be taken to signify 'many' or be used as shorthand for 'a long time'. For example, in the story of the Exodus the Israelites were in the desert for forty years; in the story of THE DELUGE it rained for forty days; in the story of the Temptation Jesus was in the wilderness for forty days.

This tomb, in the church of San Giovanni, Saluzzo, Italy, is
carved with representations of the Seven Virtues: (top, left to right)
caritas (charity), spes (hope), fide (faith), and prudentia
(prudence); (bottom, left to right) iusticia (justice),
fortitudo (fortitude), and temperantia (temperance).

If they are not in the national language, LETTERS and WORDS carved or painted in churches are almost always in or derived from Hebrew, Latin, or Ancient Greek. Hebrew is the holy language of the Old Testament, and words such as *Adonai* and *Amen* connect the church with its Old Testament roots. Latin and Ancient Greek were the 'civilized' languages of the world at the time of Jesus. Although in later centuries they ceased to be used by the general population, they continued to be used by scholars. As the Christian Church spread to different nations, Latin in particular became the medium of communication used by Churchmen. The use of Latin and Greek words in church buildings therefore shows three things: it is a link to the earliest Christians; it is a mark of intellectual understanding; and it is an expression of the communication of God's word to all the nations.

Look out for words in stained glass, fabric, carved on the walls or above the entrances to church and, of course, in art. They can appear on their own, or phrases may be abbreviated to their initial letters. It is by no means always used, but if a short horizontal line, with one end slightly lowered and one end slightly raised, appears near or over certain letters, then it is intended to indicate that the letters are an abbreviation.

We will see that some of these words are straightforward translations of key passages from the Bible. Others, such as IHC, IHS, and the Chi Rho (which, since they all indicate Jesus in some way, are known together as the Sacred Monograms), have taken on a symbolic life of their own. The more that a combination of letters has taken on this separate symbolic existence, the more likely it is to appear in combination with other symbols, such as a crown over the letters (showing Jesus' kingship), or giving off rays of light (showing Jesus' glory).

Images of the adoration of the name of Jesus – a person or group venerating the Sacred Monograms, shown shining in the night – were popular in medieval and Renaissance art.

✛

A stall-end at Altarnun Church,
near Launceston, Cornwall. The letters 'IHC', for Jesus,
are displayed on the angel's chest.

The Agnus Dei (The Lamb of God) holding a triumphal flag.
The message is that Jesus is the sacrificial lamb that has
triumphed.

Adonai Adonai

Hebrew for 'The Lord'. This was a way of referring to God while avoiding the use of his true name, which it was considered wrong to write or speak (*see* Yahweh page 127).

Agnus Dei

Latin for 'THE LAMB OF GOD' (see ST JOHN THE BAPTIST, page 209).

AMDG

AMDG stands for the Latin words *Ad Maiorem Dei Gloriam*, 'To the greater glory of God'. When the letters appear on an object, such as an item of church furniture or stained glass, it often indicates that it was donated to the church and that the donor wished that the gift would work to God's greater glory.

Amen

Amen is the Hebrew word for expressing confirmation and agreement. It means 'certainly', or 'truly', and is used in the New and Old Testaments to confirm prayers, as a statement that the preceding words are true and good. The word can also be translated as 'so be it', or 'let it be so' (Numbers 5:22), as a final plea that the prayer will be heard. In a darker twist, the word can also be used to confirm curses. MOSES decreed that *Amen* should be used by the congregation as a response to a series of curses led by the priests ('"Cursed is the man who sleeps with his mother-in-law!", then all the people shall say "Amen!" '; Deuteronomy 27:23).

AMGPD

AMGPD stands for the Latin words *Ave Maria, Gratia Plena, Dominus tecum*, 'Hail Mary, full of grace, the Lord is with you' (see THE VIRGIN MARY, page 199).

AMR

AMR stands for the Latin words *Ave Maria Regina*, 'Hail Mary, the Queen [of Heaven]'.

AΩ AΩ– *Alpha and Omega*

The first and last letters of the Greek alphabet used to indicate the beginning and the end of all things and so symbolize God, and in particular God's infinite and eternal nature. In the Book of Revelation, ST JOHN had a vision of God making this analogy himself ('I am the Alpha and the Omega,' says the Lord God, 'who is, and who was, and who is to come, the Almighty'; Revelation 1:8). Later, John saw Jesus adopting the description to himself ('I am the Alpha and the Omega, the First and the Last, the Beginning and the End'; Revelation 22:13).

The use of the alphabet's first and last letters as a symbol of God was inherited from Judaism. In the Hebrew alphabet they are *Aleph* and *Thaw*. The Hebrew word for truth is *Emeth*, a word that begins and ends with these letters. The word *Emeth* was therefore considered sacred, and to have a mystical meaning: truth was fully and infinitely in God, and there was nothing outside of him, before him, or after him, that was truth.

Look out for Greek letters high up on stained glass, when they might represent GOD THE FATHER as part of THE TRINITY (with GOD THE SPIRIT in the form of a DOVE positioned below, and GOD THE SON below that), or simply emphasize the infinity of God. They may be seen too in Jesus' HALO, over the crossbar, particularly in Eastern icons. If the letters are standing alone, they often appear with other symbols, such as a cross (to emphasize the divinity of Jesus, or the sufferings of God) or a crown (God is King of All), or the CHI RHO. Sometimes the position of the ALPHA and the OMEGA is reversed, with the Alpha on the right and the

Omega on the left. In this order, the letters show that in Jesus the beginning and the end became one.

AVE [MARIA], GRATIA PLENA, DOMINUS TECUM
Latin for 'Hail [Mary], full of grace, the Lord is with you' (Luke 1:28). See THE VIRGIN MARY and THE ANNUNCIATION (page 199).

BMV/BEATA MARIA VIRGO
'Blessed Virgin Mary'. See THE VIRGIN MARY (page 191).

✧

A stained-glass panel of Christ holding the Greek letters alpha and omega, which are used to symbolize the all-encompassing power of God, at the church of Our Lady of Walsingham, Norfolk.

DD/DDD

DD may be seen on objects donated to the church and stands for the Latin words *Donum dedit*, 'he/she gave as a gift'. A third D stands for Deo, meaning 'he/she gave as a gift to God'.

DNJC

DNJC stands for the Latin words *Dominus Noster Jesus Christus*, 'Our Lord Jesus Christ'.

DOM

DOM stands for the Latin words *Deo Optimo Maximo*, 'The highest and the greatest God' and can often be found on monuments or over church entrances. Jupiter, the king of the Roman gods, was addressed with these words, and they appear on the ruined temple of Jupiter on Rome's Capitol Hill.

Ecce Agnus Dei, qui tollit peccatum mundi

Latin: 'Behold the Lamb of God, who takes away the sin of the world' (John 1:29).

Ecce Ancilla Domini

Latin: 'Behold the handmaiden of the Lord' (Luke 1:38). See the virgin mary and the annunciation (page 199).

Ecce Homo

Latin: 'Behold the man' These were the words that Pilate used of Jesus when he presented him to the crowd (John 19:5).

Ecce Virgo Concipiet

Latin: 'Behold, the Virgin will conceive'. See the virgin mary.

Eloi, eloi, lama sabachthani?

'My God, my God, why have you forsaken me?' (Mark 15:34, from Psalm 22:1) are the words that Jesus cried out as he hung on the cross, shortly before his death. The words are Aramaic, the day-to-day language of Jesus and the disciples. They have caused difficulties for some theologians, since they seem to show Jesus the Son of God in complete despair, believing at the point of death that he had been abandoned by the very God who is meant to have been manifested in him. One explanation of the words is that at this point it was the wholly human part of Jesus that was expressing itself. They are a point of contact with Jesus that cuts like a knife through the tangle of centuries of biblical translation and exposition. This cry of pure pain, in Jesus' ordinary language, is one of the most deeply moving moments in the Bible.

HOSANNA

Hosanna is a Hebrew word meaning 'save', which developed into an exclamation of praise. It was shouted by the crowds on Jesus' ENTRY INTO JERUSALEM (page 164).

IHS AND IHC

IHS and IHC are symbols of Jesus. 'IHC' is derived from the Greek spelling of Jesus (IHCOYC). The Greeks also used the letters IH, IC or ICXC (Jesus Christ), while some of a more mystical bent used the letters IET. The letters IE were the first letters of Jesus' name, while the T formed the shape of the cross; moreover, when turned into numerals, in Greek the letters IET come to 318, a number which was thought to have a mystical significance and was the number of trained fighting men who

'IHS' intertwined in stained glass. The letters originally stood for Jesus, although as an acronym they have a number of meanings.

followed ABRAHAM, Israel's founding father (Genesis 14:14). The letters IHC were later 'translated' into the Latin form 'IHS'. Purists tend to prefer the Greek lettering because of its earlier origins. However, IHS has taken on other meanings over the years, having been mistranslated as the first letters of three separate words, variously *Iesus, Hominum Salvator* ('Jesus, Saviour of Humankind'), *Iesus Habemus Socium* ('we have Jesus as our companion'; this was the interpretation of the Jesuits, who adopted IHS as the symbol of their order), and *In Hoc Signio* ('by this sign [you shall conquer]'). These misinterpretations, if that is what they were, have given IHS a solid defence to preference over its older relative. IHS and IHC are together known as the 'Chismon'.

Immanuel/Emmanuel

Immanuel, or *Emmanuel*, means 'God with us'. First used in the Bible by the Prophet ISAIAH, who wanted to give a sign from God to stiffen the resolve of the King of Judah, King Azar, against invading armies: 'Therefore the Lord himself will give you a sign: the virgin will be with child and will give birth to a son, and will call him *Immanuel*' (Isaiah 7:14). This prophecy was applied by ST MATTHEW to Jesus (Matthew 1:22–23). The meaning for Christians is that, in Jesus, God came into the world.

INRI

You will find the letters INRI on a scroll or plaque, nailed to the top of the cross in scenes of THE CRUCIFIXION. The letters stand for '*Iesus Nazarenus Rex Iudaeorum*', Latin for 'Jesus of Nazareth, King of the Jews'. This was the inscription, in Aramaic, Greek, and Latin, that Pontius Pilate, the Roman Governor who condemned Jesus to death, had prepared and fastened to the cross. It was usual to have a placard, called the 'titulus', attached to the cross, bearing the condemned man's name and his crime. In a striking exchange, the Chief Priests complained to an unmovable Pilate that he should not have written 'the King of the Jews', but instead 'This man claimed to be the King of the Jews'. (John 19:19–22).

✛

Depictions of Christ on the Cross usually include a borad or scroll above his head with the letters 'INRI'. Stained-glass window at the church of St Thomas, Heptonstall, West Yorkshire.

JHVH (Jehovah)/YHWH (Yahweh)

When God appeared to MOSES in THE BURNING BUSH, Moses asked him what he should tell the Israelites was God's name. God replied, 'I AM WHO I AM. This is what you are to say to the Israelites: "I AM has sent me to you"' (Exodus 3:14). This was an expression that God is complete and self-existent. In Hebrew the word is *Yahweh* and in Jewish tradition the name of God was too sacred to speak or write, so it was substituted by the word *Adonai* ('Lord') and written in consonants YHWH. In later transcriptions of the Bible, YHWH became JHVH, and, in the Middle Ages, the vowels from *Adonai* were added to JHVH, to give the name of God as *Jehovah*.

M/MR/Mater Dei (ma di/MP OY)

The letter 'M' is likely to refer to THE VIRGIN MARY. This can appear with an 'R' (for MaRia, or *Maria Regina*). When the two letters are joined, with the loop of the 'R' piercing the right hand arm of the 'M' the arrangement is known as the Monogram of the Blessed Virgin. As with the Sacred Monograms, these letters can be combined with other symbols to give particular meanings, such as a crown to show that Mary is Queen of Heaven.

MHP.OY

This is an abbreviation of *Meter Theou*, Greek for 'Mother of God'. It is found on Orthodox icons of THE VIRGIN MARY.

N/Nika

Greek word meaning 'victor', or 'conqueror' sometimes combined with the CHI RHO or the letters IC or IC XC to represent the phrase 'Jesus, Victor' or 'Christ, Conqueror', a reference to Jesus' victory over death and sin. Sometimes only the 'N' for *Noster* is used, superimposed over a Sacred Monogram or a cross, softening the meaning to 'Our Jesus'.

Noli Me Tangere

Latin: 'Do not touch me' (John 20:14). See ST MARY MAGDALENE (page 213)

Quo Vadis?/Domine Quo Vadis?

Latin: 'Where are you going? Lord, where are you going?' See ST PETER (page 220).

RIP

The letters RIP, familiar from gravestones and funeral monuments, stand for the Latin *Requiescat In Pace*, or equally nowadays its English translation, 'Rest In Peace'. It expresses the hope and wishes of the living for the dead person's peace, and acts as a prayer for them.

Sanctus Sanctus Sanctus

'Holy, Holy, Holy'. These were the words sung endlessly by the mystical creatures around the throne of God, in ST JOHN'S vision (Revelation 4:7–8). They may also be sung by the congregation during THE EUCHARIST. See THE FOUR EVANGELISTS (page 217).

Sta.

Sta. is an abbreviation of *Santa*, meaning 'saint'.

VDMA/Verbum Dei Manet in Aeternum

Latin: 'The Word of God endures for ever' (1 Peter 1:25). Look out for the letters or words on or around places where the Bible is read out in church, such as LECTERNS or PULPITS. They are sometimes portrayed in imagery as printed in a book, in which case the book is meant to be the Bible.

Vox clamantis in deserto

Latin: 'A voice crying out in the wilderness' (Mark 1:3).

XP – the Chi Rho

THE CHI RHO is, with the letters 'IHS' or 'IHC', one of the Sacred Monograms. 'XP' stands for 'Christ', from the Greek word for Christ, XPICTOC. The symbol is known as the Chi Rho, after the names for the Greek letters.
In signifying the word 'Christ' rather than 'Jesus', the emphasis in the symbol is on Jesus' position as the Son of God, the Messiah. The 'X' in the Chi Rho can be used artistically as a reminder of the cross, and so the letters are often interlinked to make a single whole.

A stylized Chi Rho, depicted in stained glass.

Like so much Christian symbolism, the Chi Rho has a meaning that predates Christianity. The Ancient Greek word for gold (*chrysoun*) starts with the same two letters, and the Chi Rho was stamped onto coins to show that they were made of gold. This meaning pleased Greek Christians, as the symbol represented their golden Christ.

The popularity of the symbol soared after it was adopted in 312 by the Emperor Constantine, the first Christian Roman Emperor, who, the night before a battle, had a dream in which

Chi Rho, with Emperor Constantine

Jesus appeared to him and told him to place the Chi Rho, together with the words *En toutoi nika* ('By this sign, you will conquer'), on his military standards. Despite overwhelming odds. he defeated the Emperor Maxentius and went on to declare Christianity the state religion. In the course of the fourth century the sign was stamped onto everything from tombs to household utensils.

✛

An altar frontal embroidered with the Chi Rho and the letters alpha and omega, at the church of St Botolph, Boston, Lincolnshire.

GREEN is the colour of new life. As a liturgical colour, it is a kind of 'default' setting, used whenever the other colours are not. PURPLE is the colour used for seasons of repentance. In the Western Church, the ecclesiastical year starts with the penitential season of Advent, which runs for four Sundays from the fourth Sunday before Christmas (so, from around 1 December). It is a period of preparation and anticipation (the name Advent comes from *Adventus Domini*, 'the coming of the Lord'), before the Christmas celebration of Jesus' birth and anticipation of his return. The second period of penance in which purple is used is Lent. Lent (the name has the same root as 'lengthen', and is a reference to the lengthening days of the time of year) is the forty-day period of repentance and preparation in the lead-up to the most important Christian festival, Easter.

WHITE is the liturgical colour of both Christmas and Easter. The white of the church furnishings remains through the twelve days of Christmas, and through the festival and season of Epiphany, 6 January and the following four Sundays. Epiphany comes from the Greek *epiphanmeia*, 'to shine upon', 'show', or 'manifest', and is the celebration of God's manifestation of Himself. In the West the festival that marks this is the VISIT OF THE MAGI (when Jesus was first revealed to the Gentiles), and in the East it is THE BAPTISM OF JESUS (when the ministry of Jesus began), and also the wedding at Cana (when Jesus performed his first miracle). White is used again at the greatest Christian festival, Easter, in celebration of THE RESURRECTION. On the seven Sundays after Easter, white is also used, until Ascension Day, forty days after Easter, when THE ASCENSION is commemorated. The last day on which white is used is Trinity Sunday. The day honours all three persons of THE TRINITY – GOD THE FATHER, GOD THE SON and GOD THE HOLY SPIRIT – and summarizes the whole of God's revelation to humankind.

The traditional interpretations of colours in church art are as follows:

BLACK

Sickness, death, and the devil, but also mourning. BLACK is sometimes used as a liturgical colour of mourning on Good

Friday. Black and white together, though, can represent purity, for example on the habits of Dominican friars.

BLUE
Traditionally associated with THE VIRGIN MARY, and also with Jesus, BLUE is the colour of the sky and represents heavenly love.

BROWN
The simple dress of the Franciscans is brown, in imitation of poor peasant dress. BROWN came to represent renunciation of the world.

GOLD
GOLD is the colour of light, and has the same symbolic meanings as WHITE, with which it is often used.

GREEN
GREEN is the colour of life, and in particular the triumph of life over death, just as green spring overcomes winter.

GREY
The colour of ashes, GREY symbolizes the death of the body, repentance, and humility. In paintings of THE LAST JUDGEMENT, Jesus is sometimes shown wearing grey.

Detail of a stained-glass window at the church of the Holy Trinity, Wensley, North Yorkshire.

IT *IS* FINISHED

Purple

In addition to its liturgical function as the colour of penance, PURPLE represents royalty, and was the colour of Imperial power. For this reason, GOD THE FATHER is sometimes shown in a purple mantle.

Red

RED is the fire of PENTECOST, also known as Whitsun (because it was the custom to baptize on that Sunday, when WHITE clothes had to be worn). The red remembers the fire, when the Holy Spirit came to the Apostles, and the day is known as the birthday of the Church. Red is also the colour of the passions. It can mean hate or love, although it is most often used for the latter. For example, MARY MAGDALENE is often shown in red to illustrate her love, and in images of THE SACRED HEART, when the onlooker is invited to meditate on Jesus' spirit, Jesus is often dressed in a red cloak. As the colour of blood, red is also often used for the clothes of martyrs and in flowers at scenes of martyrdom.

White

The Bible contains several references to WHITE as the colour of purity and innocence (for example, 'wash me, and I shall be whiter than snow', Psalm 51:37). It also shows spiritual transcendence: Jesus' clothes became dazzling white during THE TRANSFIGURATION (Matthew 17:2), and the ANGELS at THE RESURRECTION were dressed in white (Matthew 28:3). When the risen Jesus is portrayed, he is usually shown dressed in white. Silver can be used instead of white.

Yellow

YELLOW can be used as a variant of WHITE to represent light, and is a common colour for HALOS in stained glass. It can, though, also indicate an infernal light of treachery and deceit. Yellow was used in the Middle Ages to mark out plague areas, and so it came to suggest contagion and impurity. For this reason, JUDAS ISCARIOT is sometimes portrayed wearing yellow.

✣

The Virgin Mary at the foot of the Cross surrounded by roses, one of her identifying attributes. St Luke's Church, Norland, near Sowerby, West Yorkshire.

REPRESENTATIONS 4
OF GOD

'Thou shalt not make thee any graven image' (Deuteronomy 5:8–9) commands the second of THE TEN COMMANDMENTS, creating a clear break between pagan worship, which was thought to be directed at specific idols, and the way the Jewish God would be worshipped: no idols necessary. As we will see, the commandment has inhibited direct portrayals of GOD THE FATHER, although this has meant that this is an area in which symbolism has come into its own. We will be looking at ways in which the three persons of God – Father, Son, and Spirit – are represented in churches, and how they are used to illustrate specifically Christian teachings about God.

THE TRINITY is a central dogma in Eastern and Western Churches about the nature of God. God is at the same time one substance and three distinct, separate persons: God the Father, God the Son and God the Holy Spirit. As they are one God, the three do not have different 'roles' as such but, broadly speaking, the Father might be thought of as the creator and preserver of the world, the Son is the intellect and the Word of God manifested in Jesus, and the Spirit fills people, touching the disciples at PENTECOST and still working in people today. The three stand equal, eternal, omnipotent - and one.

✥

The Trinity enthroned in glory: God the Father with a seven-pointed halo, God the Son with a cruciform halo, and God the Holy Spirit, in the form of a dove and (above) 'The virtue of Silence'.

Equilateral Triangle

Two Triangles

Triangle in Circle

Symbols of THE TRINITY always involve the number three. An equilateral triangle is one of the oldest Christian symbols, the equality of the sides and the angles expressing the equality of the Persons of the Trinity. Two interwoven triangles forming a six-pointed star can also be used. This image has a theological message, with a special reference to THE CREATION: a six-pointed star is an ancient symbol of creation, and using two interlacing triangles expresses the eternal nature of the Trinity, since it was present at the Creation.

Circles are a symbol of God and the equilateral triangle is often portrayed with a circle inside or outside it. Three interwoven circles represent the Trinity, as do the three-pointed symbols known as the trefoil and the triqueta. In fact, any three objects woven together are likely to symbolize the Trinity, most commonly three FISH.

A three-petalled flower such as the fleur-de-lys is often used to represent the Trinity, as is the CLOVER or shamrock. The latter comes from a legend of St Patrick, a missionary to the Irish and now Ireland's patron saint. When challenged about the doctrine of the Trinity, Patrick plucked a shamrock from the ground and asked his listeners whether he held one leaf or three. Having stunned his audience into silence, Patrick said that if they could not understand the shamrock, then how could they expect to understand the Trinity?

A heraldic shield (the 'Shield of the Blessed Trinity') is sometimes used, particularly in churches dedicated to the Holy Trinity. The Latin words *Pater* (Father), *Filius* (Son), and *Spiritus*

The Trinity: Father, Son, and Holy Spirit

A double Trinity star, enclosing the rose of the Virgin Mary, in the chancel at the church of Holy Trinity, Low Moor, near Bradford, West Yorkshire.

(Spirit) stand in a triangle, with *Deus* (God) in the middle of them. The words *non est* (is not) runs between each of the words *Pater*, *Filius*, and *Spiritus*, to show that the Father 'is not' the Son, who in turn 'is not' the Spirit. The word *est* (is) runs between the word *Deus* and the other three words, to express the idea that, nevertheless, the Father is God, the Son is God, and the Spirit is God.

GOD THE FATHER

It may seem surprising, but the cartoon image of God, as an ancient white-haired man sitting on a throne, does have biblical authority. The Prophet DANIEL had a vision of God like a man sitting on a throne, 'whose garment was white as snow, and the hair of his head like the pure wool: his throne was like the fiery flame, and his wheels as burning fire' (Daniel 7:9). However, there has traditionally been some reluctance to portray God in a representational way, because of the prohibition against creating idols in the second of THE TEN COMMANDMENTS. This prohibition was sometimes interpreted as also forbidding the creation of an image of God.

God may, though, be represented symbolically. The most common symbol is a hand - always the right - known as the *Manus Dei* ('Hand of God'), which emerges from a cloud in a blaze of light, or is circled with a cruciform HALO. Different shapes and directions of the hand indicate different intentions. If the hand is extending downwards towards humankind, then it expresses God's grace; two fingers extended indicates God's blessing; an open palm, God's assistance; and an arrangement with the first finger extended, the second and fourth curved, and the thumb and third finger crossed expresses Jesus, because it spells ICXC. When the hand is shown holding a number of small figures, it signifies God is holding the souls of the righteous, after the Book of Wisdom ('the Souls of the Righteous are in the hand of God').

Letters can be used, often within a circle, triangle, or blaze of glory. These may be the Hebrew letters for Yahweh, or, since the name of Yahweh was considered too holy to use, one or two yods (yods are the Hebrew letters that form part of 'Yahweh'). Alternatively, the words *El Saddai* (the Almighty) or *Adonai* (Lord) are used. Other symbolic representations of GOD THE FATHER are an eye, to express God's omnipotence and all-seeing nature, a cloud, or an aureole standing alone.

✥

God the Father, after the vision of the Prophet Daniel. The detail is from an image of the Crucifixion with God the Holy Spirit also present in the form of a dove in front of the letters 'INRI' (p. 127).

Needless to say, images of Jesus usually appear all about in churches. This section deals with individual symbols and representations, while the next, 'Jesus', deals with episodes from his life. Other symbols that can refer to Jesus include the sun, the star, the branch, the fountain, the VINE, the PELICAN, and the SNAKE.

Fish

The FISH is an ancient Christian symbol, predating even the cross as a sign used by the early Christians. The Greek word for fish is *icthus*, which can be read as an acronym of the Greek phrase *Iesous Christos Theou Huios Soter* ('Jesus Christ, Son of God, Saviour'). It may be that the early Christians adopted this because it was a secret symbol, which would not draw attention to them at a time when the Church was suffering persecution.

Lamb of God (Agnus Dei)

'LAMB OF GOD' is a description of Jesus first used by ST JOHN THE BAPTIST. When John first saw Jesus he cried out, 'Behold the Lamb of God, who takes away the sin of the world!' (John 1:29). The image is taken up in Acts ('He was led like a sheep to the slaughter, and as a lamb before the shearer is silent, so he did not open his mouth', Acts 8:32 and Isaiah 53:7), by ST PETER ('Christ, a lamb without blemish or defect', 1 Peter 1:20), by ST PAUL (Jesus is 'our Passover lamb', 1 Corinthians 5:7), and by ST JOHN the Divine ('Worthy is the Lamb, who was slain, to receive power and wealth and wisdom and strength and honour and glory and praise!', Revelation 5:12). A lamb that represents Jesus is identifiable by its cruciform HALO.

The image is one of meekness and suffering (going quietly to the slaughter), and of purity, through the whiteness of a lamb's fleece. Above all, the image is of Jesus as a sacrificial lamb, and specifically a lamb sacrificed at the Jewish ceremony of Passover.

⁂

Christ in Glory, on the altar frontal in the crypt of Liverpool Roman Catholic Cathedral. 'Ego sum via veritas et vita' is from John 14:6: 'I am the way, the truth and the life.'

EGO TAS
SVM ET
VIA VITA
VERI IOAN
XIV·VI

In the story of THE EXODUS, God planned to compel Pharaoh to release the people of Israel from slavery by killing the firstborn of each Egyptian household. He told the people of Israel to sacrifice lambs and use their blood to mark their doorposts, so that by that sign God would know to pass over their homes, and not take their firstborn. In John's Gospel, Jesus' death mirrors God's commands as to how to carry out this sacrifice: Jesus died at twilight on Passover, the time God told the Israelites that lambs should be sacrificed (John 19:4/Exodus 12:6); Jesus was offered wine from hyssop, a hairy plant that retained the liquid it was dipped in, just as God told the Israelites to dip hyssop in the blood of the sacrificed lambs (John 19:29/Exodus 12:22); and Jesus' bones were not broken, just as God told the Israelites not to break the bones of the sacrificial lambs (John 19:36/Exodus 12:46). On this reading, Jesus is the ultimate Passover sacrifice, causing God to pass over and spare humankind.

The lamb is often shown in a position of triumph, standing with its leg hooked around the pole of a flag made up of a red cross on a white background and topped with another cross (English public houses often have names that derive from religious imagery – the Lamb and Flag is just one example). The image is meant to convey the message that Jesus is the sacrifice that has triumphed. The lamb may also be shown bleeding into a cup, which is Jesus' blood becoming the wine of the Eucharist.

A lamb (or RAM) also appears in Jewish writing about the apocalypse at the end of time, as the agent of God who would crush evil and save God's people. This is the starting-point for the use of a lamb in St John's vision in the Book of Revelation. John

saw a lamb, and a book with seven seals. When the lamb opened the seals, it ushered in the final apocalypse. If a lamb is positioned on or beside a book from which seven seals are hanging, it is a reference to this terrifying vision (Revelation 5).

✣

*John the Baptist holding the Lamb of God (*Agnus Dei*).*
Detail from a stained-glass window at the church of
St Giles, Cheadle, Staffordshire.

THE SACRED HEART

A common devotional image in Roman Catholic and some Anglican churches is that of THE SACRED HEART. The heart may be rayed, or on fire, topped with a small cross or crown, pierced with a spear, or ringed by a CROWN OF THORNS. In some images, Jesus looks directly at the onlooker, holding open his cloak with one hand to reveal his heart beneath. The image focuses on Jesus' inner spirit and is intended for use by the onlooker as an object of meditation or a channel for worship. Above all, it is Jesus' love and his courage that are remembered in images of the Sacred Heart, with the rays or fire emphasizing the strength of his passion.

The biblical basis for the image is the wound that Jesus received in his side when a Roman soldier speared him as he hung on the cross. There was a steady increase in theological meditations on Jesus' wounds and his heart from around the twelfth century. The image received its greatest boost, though, through the visions of St Mary Margaret (1647–90), a nun at the Visitation Convent at Paray-le-Monial in France. She was an ascetic who had received visions of Jesus from an early age. These visions began gradually to focus on the Sacred Heart. Jesus told Mary Margaret that he wanted to be honoured through the image of a heart, and in June 1675 Jesus appeared to her with the words 'Behold the Heart that has so loved men'. Mary Margaret was persuaded to write an account of her visions, which quickly became popular.

Similar images of the heart are also attributed to THE VIRGIN MARY, when they are known as the Immaculate Heart of Mary. They can be distinguished from the Sacred Heart of Jesus, because whereas the heart of Jesus is pierced with a spear, the heart of Mary is pierced with a sword. The image derives from Mary's meeting with Simeon at THE PRESENTATION. Taking the baby Jesus in his arms, Simeon turned to Mary and said, 'This child is destined to cause the falling and rising of many in Israel, and to be a sign that will be spoken against, so that the thoughts of many hearts will be revealed. And a sword will pierce your own soul too' (Luke 2:25–35).

✢

'Behold the heart that has so loved men': images of the
Sacred Heart depict Jesus' spirit, love and courage.

GLORY · TO · GOD

GOD THE HOLY
SPIRIT/HOLY GHOST

The most common way of representing THE HOLY SPIRIT is in the form of a DOVE. The reference comes from THE BAPTISM OF JESUS: 'When all the people were being baptized, Jesus was baptized too. And as he was praying, heaven was opened and the Holy Spirit descended on him in bodily form like a dove. And a voice came from heaven: "You are my Son, whom I love; with you I am well pleased" ' (Luke 3:21–22). Look out for the dove high up on the main stained-glass window, where it is often to be seen descending and haloed (frequently with a cruciform HALO).

The Holy Spirit can also be represented by fire, in particular a fire with seven or nine or twelve tongues of flame, or by seven or nine hanging lamps, or an equal number of doves. The reference to fire is to PENTECOST. The disciples were sitting in a room together, when there was suddenly a sound like a violent wind, and tongues of fire appeared and touched each of them. The disciples were filled with the Holy Spirit and began to speak in other languages (Acts 2:1–4). The reference to the hanging lamps is to the gifts of the Holy Spirit, and this is also the origin of the different numberings. If there are seven lamps, tongues of fire, or doves, then they represent the seven 'sanctifying' gifts of the Holy Spirit: wisdom (*sapientia*), understanding (*intellectus*), counsel (*consilium*), spiritual strength (*fortitudo*), knowledge (*scientia*), godliness (*pietas*), and fear of God (*timor*) (derived from Isaiah 11:2–3). If there are nine, then they represent the nine 'charismatic' gifts: speaking with wisdom, speaking with knowledge, faith, the power of healing, the power to perform miracles, the power to prophesy, the gift of discerning spirits, speaking in tongues, and the gift of interpreting (derived from 1 Corinthians 12:8–10). There may be twelve tongues of fire, because at PENTECOST the fire of the Holy Spirit touched each of the twelve disciples.

✣

Window showing the cross along with a dove descending, representing the Holy Spirit; Wesleyan Methodist chapel, Gledholt, Huddersfield, West Yorkshire.

REPRESENTATIONS 6 OF JESUS

There are few churches that do not contain many images of Jesus, in stained glass, on the walls, in paintings, statues, or on crucifixes. The way he is portrayed has developed over time. The earliest representations portrayed him as a young man, clean-shaven and with long curling hair. The now-familiar image of Jesus, bearded and in his early thirties, derives from an

Mary and Jesus, with monograms

apocryphal description that was supposedly sent to the Roman Senate by Publius Lentulus, Proconsul of Judaea, after a meeting with Jesus. Lentulus described Jesus as having hair that was straight from his crown to his ears before descending in curls to his shoulders and then down his back, where it was divided into two portions. He said that Jesus had an abundant forked beard, and that his hair was the colour of wine (a description that is not terribly helpful, given the variety of wine's colours). Whether Lentulus' description was true, or is a fiction created from a desire to know more about Jesus' appearance, it was in circulation among the early Christians, and from the fourth century the Emperor Constantine, the first Christian Roman Emperor, commissioned images of Jesus to be made on the basis of it.

✛

The image of Christ on St Veronica's cloth, from a Greek Orthodox manuscript and (above) a mosaic icon of the Virgin and Child at the church of St Maria in Cosmedin, Rome.

A teaching that was hotly debated in the early centuries of Christianity concerned the exact nature of Jesus. Was he a man, a prophet? Or was he God, descended to earth? The conclusion the Church reached was that Jesus was both wholly human, and wholly God. Specifically, Jesus was the incarnation (from the Latin *incarnatio*, 'made flesh') of GOD THE SON, the second person of THE TRINITY. References to this 'dual nature' are frequent in imagery.

Apologies to bearded readers for what follows. Images of Jesus with a beard may also have developed through a wish to symbolize ugliness. There was some debate in the early Church as to whether Jesus was in appearance the most handsome, or the most repulsive, of men. One view was that since God is supremely beautiful, and Jesus was God on earth, so Jesus too must have been supremely beautiful. The opposing view was that God the Son took on himself all human misery when he entered the world, and so had a horrible, diseased appearance. This 'ugly' view claimed support from the Prophet ISAIAH: 'he had … nothing in his appearance that we should desire him. He was despised and rejected by others … surely he has borne our infirmities and carried our diseases' (Isaiah 53:2–4). Bearded and unbearded images of Jesus appeared concurrently until around the eleventh century. The theory runs that during this period, if an artist wanted to emphasize Jesus' divinity then he would take the 'beauty' side of the debate, and symbolize this by having Jesus beardless, whereas he would portray him as bearded if he wanted to emphasize Jesus' humanity and supposed ugliness. From around the eleventh century, images of Jesus with a beard took the ascendance.

We now turn to representations of some scenes from the life of Jesus. There is a tendency in church imagery to portray events that are marked by a Church festival, which in turn tend to mark events in the early and later stages of his life. Therefore what follows has an emphasis on those events, rather than aspects of Jesus' ministry and teaching. Jesus is the focal point of every scene in which he appears, and is often identifiable by his cruciform HALO.

✣

Detail of a stained-glass window illustrating the Presentation of Jesus by Simeon in the Temple, at the church of St Thomas Apostle, Heptonstall, West Yorkshire.

THE NATIVITY

The Bible states that Jesus was born in a stable in Bethlehem. The key figures in any NATIVITY scene are the baby Jesus, who lies or sits on a bed of straw or in a manger; his mother THE VIRGIN MARY, dressed in blue; his foster father, ST JOSEPH, bearded and usually in brown; and an OX and an ASS.

The ox and the ass do not appear in the Gospels, but derive from the opening chapter of Isaiah: 'The ox knows his master, the donkey his owner's manger, but Israel does not know, my people do not understand' (Isaiah 1:3). Apocryphal Gospels later recorded their presence as fact. Some Christian commentators tried to explain how the ox and the ass came to be there: the ox, they said, was brought to Bethlehem by Joseph to sell, while the ass was transport for Mary.

To be biblically correct, Jesus should appear wrapped tightly in cloth. However, many artists felt that it would make a more affecting scene to portray Jesus out of these constraints. In 1370 the mystic St Brigid of Sweden had a famous vision of the Nativity, which also influenced portrayals. Brigid saw an 'instantaneous' birth in which Jesus was born radiant in glory and free of constraints, while Mary fell on her knees before him in welcome and worship. In an alternative account of the birth, from another fourteenth-century work, *Meditations on the Life of Christ*, Mary gave birth standing up and leaning on a column.

The stable is often portrayed as a tumble-down building. This may be a symbol of the dilapidation of the old covenant with God, which was now to be replaced by a new covenant through Jesus, or it may be another tradition from the *Meditations*, that the family rested in a shelter that Joseph had built. The stable has also been portrayed as a cave, after certain of the apocryphal Gospels. The Holy Family may be joined by a group of shepherds, and one or more of their SHEEP (a reminder of Jesus as the LAMB OF GOD). The shepherds went to visit the new king after ANGELS appeared to them outside Jerusalem to announce the birth of the Messiah.

✧

Madonna and child, St Mary's, Happisburgh, Norfolk

THE MAGI

Matthew's Gospel records that the Holy Family was visited by THE MAGI, who had observed a star in the east and come looking for the King of the Jews. In the Bible the Magi are wise men or astrologers, although they are usually portrayed as kings, a portrayal that derives from the idea that their visit fulfilled prophecies in the Psalms that 'all kings shall fall down before him' (72:11), and in ISAIAH that 'Nations shall come to your light, and kings to the brightness of your dawn' (60:3–6). One significance of the visit in Christian teaching is that the Magi were the first non-Jews to recognize Jesus. In addition, the fact that the Magi bowed down before Jesus was often cited by the Church as proof of the submission of earthly powers to its heavenly power.

The Magi did not arrive until after THE PRESENTATION. Matthew's Gospel refers to them visiting the Holy Family in a house, rather than in the stable (2:11), and they may have visited up to two years after THE NATIVITY. Jesus is therefore often older in scenes including the Magi than he is in scenes of the Nativity. The Magi brought with them symbolic gifts of gold, frankincense, and myrrh. Gold was later interpreted as representing Jesus' kingship, frankincense (an incense used in worship) his divinity or priestliness, and myrrh (an embalmer for the dead) his death. There is no record in the Bible of how many Magi there were, but the number of gifts led to three being portrayed. Their traditional names in the West are Gaspar (or Caspar, who is the oldest, and bearded), Melchior, and Balthasar. From the fourteenth century the Magi were sometimes portrayed as being of different races, with Balthasar, carrier of myrrh, portrayed as having been black. This came from the idea that all the races of the earth – European, Asian, and African – had come to worship the new King (Matthew 2:1–12).

✛

One of the Magi, surrounded by flowers,
depicted in a stained-glass window at St Leonard's Church,
Colchester, Essex.

REPRESENTATIONS OF JESUS

THE BAPTISM OF JESUS

ST JOHN THE BAPTIST was preaching repentance in the Judaean desert, and baptizing those that came to him. Jesus came to be baptized. As John baptized him 'heaven was opened, and he saw the Spirit of God descending like a dove and lighting on him. And a voice from heaven said, "This is my Son, whom I love; with him I am well pleased." ' This point is considered to be the start of Jesus' ministry.

Representations of the baptism usually have Jesus wearing a loincloth and standing in the River Jordan. John pours water over his head, as light streams from the heavens or GOD THE FATHER appears (for example, represented by a hand) and GOD THE HOLY SPIRIT descends in the form of a DOVE. If there are FISH in the water, these represent Christian souls: the water of baptism gives them 'new life', just as water is life to the fish. ANGELS sometimes appear on the bank of the river, holding

Jesus' clothes. Either Jesus or John may be kneeling before the other. If John is kneeling, it is an allusion to his humbling himself before Jesus, with the words 'I need to be baptized by you, and do you come to me?' (Matthew 3:14). If Jesus is kneeling, it is meant to indicate his humility in accepting a ritual of purification that was unnecessary, since Jesus was without sin.

✛

Detail of a stained-glass window at Hellington Church, Norfolk, depicting the baptism of Jesus by St John the Baptist, whose words, 'Behold the Lamb of God' (John 1:29), appear on the banner.

The Massacre of the Innocents

On their way to Bethlehem, THE MAGI had told Herod that they were looking for the King of the Jews, who was to be born in Bethlehem. Disturbed by this apparent threat to his power, Herod asked the Magi to tell him once they had found this King. However, after the Magi had visited Jesus, they were warned in a dream to return home by a different route. Incensed, Herod gave an order that every boy in Bethlehem and its vicinity under the age of two should be put to death (Matthew 2:13–15). These 'Holy Innocents' have been considered the first Christian martyrs, dying in place of Jesus. A medieval convention portrayed them being killed before the throne of Herod.

The Flight to Egypt

Jesus was saved because an ANGEL appeared to Joseph and told him to escape with his family to Egypt. An image of Joseph leading an ASS on which Mary is carrying the infant Jesus, possibly guarded by one or more angels, is a representation of THE FLIGHT INTO EGYPT. Interesting traditions grew up around the Flight. A broken or tottering building in images of the Flight comes from the story that the pagan idols of the Temple of Sotinen in Egypt fell to the ground when Mary and Jesus arrived and entered it. The tradition is derived from a prophecy of Isaiah, 'See, the Lord is riding on a swift cloud and comes to Egypt, the idols of Egypt will tremble at his presence' (Isaiah 19:1). A bending tree alludes to another story, from the apocryphal Gospel of pseudo-Matthew. On the journey Mary wished to eat the fruit of a tall tree beneath which the family was resting. On Jesus' command the tree bent down to give its fruit into Mary's hand. Other background images might include a cornfield, in which the corn has miraculously ripened overnight, or sowers and reapers

The Return from Egypt

After the death of King Herod, an ANGEL told JOSEPH that the land was now safe. Joseph therefore returned with his family to Nazareth, in fulfilment of a prophecy that the Messiah would come from Nazareth (Matthew 2:19–23). THE RETURN FROM EGYPT was also significant because of its reflection of THE EXODUS. Images of the return from Egypt differ from those of THE FLIGHT TO EGYPT, because Jesus is portrayed as a young boy.

Christ among the Doctors
Dispute in the Temple

Each year Mary and JOSEPH went to the Temple in Jerusalem for the Feast of the Passover. Returning from the feast when Jesus was twelve, they accidentally left him behind. They returned to Jerusalem, and after three days found Jesus in the Temple, deep in discussion with the teachers (rabbis). The scene is significant in Christian terms for a number of reasons. It shows Jesus' precocious abilities; it is the first instance of Jesus teaching; and it is the first time that Jesus indicated his position as the Son of God, through his rebuke to his worried mother ('Why were you searching for me? Didn't you know I had to be in my Father's house?' Luke 2:49).

The teachers can be portrayed in exotic Eastern dress and turbans, although the scene is sometimes given a contemporary spin by putting them in modern scholarly dress. Sometimes Jesus is portrayed holding a book, while one of the teachers is holding a scroll – an arrangement that is intended to contrast the New and Old Testaments.

✦ The Raising of Lazarus

LAZARUS, the brother of Mary (possibly ST MARY MAGDALENE) and Martha, fell sick and died. By the time Jesus arrived at the tomb, Lazarus had been dead for four days. Jesus comforted Martha with words that are used in the funeral service, and may appear on representations of the scene: 'I am the resurrection and the life. He who believes in me will live, even though he dies; and whoever lives and believes in me will never die' (John 11:25-26).

Mary then fell weeping at Jesus' feet, and 'Jesus wept' (words famous as the shortest verse in the Bible: John 11:35). Jesus then ordered that the stone be removed from the entrance to Lazarus' tomb, in spite of Martha's protest, 'Lord, by this time he stinketh' (Mary and Martha are sometimes shown holding their noses). Jesus then called in a loud voice, 'Lazarus, come out!' The dead man came out, his hands and feet wrapped with strips of linen, and a cloth around his face (John 11:1–44).

THE TRANSFIGURATION

Jesus went with ST PETER, ST JOHN, and ST JAMES onto a mountain (traditionally Mt Tabor in Galilee) to pray. As he prayed, the appearance of his face changed, and his clothes became bright as a flash of lightning. MOSES and Elijah then appeared, talking with Jesus. The three disciples, who had been sleeping, woke up, and Peter offered to build three shelters for them. While he was speaking, they were enveloped by a cloud from which a voice came, saying, 'This is my Son, whom I have chosen; listen to him.' After the voice had spoken, they found that Jesus was alone (Luke 9:28–36). The scene is important as a manifestation of Jesus' future glory, rather like the trailer to a film.

EXPULSION OF THE MONEYCHANGERS

Strictly speaking, the EXPULSION OF THE MONEYCHANGERS, or the Cleansing of the Temple, took place after Jesus had entered Jerusalem. However, since it does not form part of the Passion cycle, it is usually treated separately.

Jesus entered the Temple area, and with a scourge of small cords began furiously driving out those who were buying and selling there, overturning the tables of the moneychangers (who converted Roman coins, which could not be used in the Temple, into kosher money, which could) and the benches of those selling OXEN, SHEEP, and DOVES for sacrifice. Jesus gave the reason for his uncharacteristic behaviour: 'Is it not written: "My house will be called a house of prayer for all nations" But you have made it a den of robbers' (Mark 11:15–17; John 2:13). Jesus is generally shown brandishing his scourge, in the middle of a chaos of spilt coins, escaping animals, and cowering people.

✛

*The Raising of Lazarus carved onto
the capital of a pillar, at the church of San
Juan de la Peña, Spain*

THE ENTRY INTO JERUSALEM

The events of the last week of Jesus' life are known as the Passion. They begin with Jesus' triumphal entry, after preaching through Judaea, into Jerusalem. He entered the city riding on a young ASS that the disciples had collected for him. Jesus' fame preceded him, and many spread their cloaks on the road, or PALMS or branches cut in the field (if palms are not shown, the branches are usually olives, in reference to the Mount of Olives, where Jesus was to be betrayed). John's Gospel explains that the entry on a DONKEY was a fulfilment of the words of the Prophet Zechariah: 'Do not be afraid, daughter of Zion. Look, your king is coming, sitting on a donkey's colt!' (Zechariah 9:9; John 12:15). Jesus is usually shown entering the city gates, from (bad) left to (good) right. Riding side-saddle is a normal way in Palestine to travel on a donkey, and in the Eastern Church this is how Jesus is shown riding.

The crowds shouted words that may appear near the representations of the scene: 'Hosanna! Blessed is he who comes in the name of the Lord!' Sometimes a large number of children are included in the crowd. This may come from a passage in the apocryphal Gospel of Nicodemus, that at the coming of Jesus 'the children of the Hebrews held branches in their hands'; it may also be a reference to the choirboys who might greet or lead the congregation as it processed into church, carrying their palms, on Palm Sunday.

Often appearing in the scene is the little figure of Zacchaeus up a tree, although strictly speaking his story took place in Jericho, and not in Jerusalem. Zacchaeus was a wealthy tax collector. A short man, he could not see Jesus over the crowds, and so he climbed a sycamore tree beside which Jesus was to walk. Jesus saw him, told him to come down, and said that he was coming to stay at his house (Mark 11:1–11; Luke 19:1–10 & 28–40).

✣

Jesus enters Jerusalem from (bad) left to (good) right. People carry palm branches and spread their cloaks and the leafy branches that they had cut in the field.

THE LAST SUPPER

Jesus' words and deeds during his LAST SUPPER with his disciples before his betrayal and death are the basis of THE EUCHARIST, the Church's central act of worship. Images of the Last Supper are therefore extremely common in churches, particularly behind or above the altar, where the Eucharist is celebrated.

The meal of the Last Supper was held in celebration of the Passover, the festival that commemorates the liberation of Israel in THE EXODUS. Jesus and the disciples ate together in a large upstairs room. During the meal, Jesus said that one of the disciples would betray him. ST JOHN was reclining beside Jesus, and asked who he meant (John 13:23–27). Jesus revealed to JUDAS ISCARIOT (although not to the other disciples) that he knew that it would be him, by dipping a sop of bread in wine and handing it to him (John's Gospel), or alternatively by dipping his bread into a bowl at the same time as Judas (Mark's and Matthew's Gospels). Although the group would have been eating lamb (since it was Passover), sometimes the table is shown laid with FISH. The fish is a symbol of Jesus, and was also associated with miraculous feeding because of its use in the feeding of the five thousand, which some Christian writers thought anticipated the Eucharist.

While they were eating, Jesus performed the ceremony that remains central to the Eucharist. He took bread, gave thanks and broke it, and gave it to his disciples, saying, 'Take and eat; this is my body.' Then he took the cup, gave thanks, and offered it to them, saying, 'Drink from it, all of you. This is my blood of the covenant, which is poured out for many for the forgiveness of sins.' (Matthew 26:17–30; Mark 14:12–26; Luke 22:7–22.) These words may be inscribed near the scene.

Representations of the Last Supper usually include the twelve disciples seated around the table, with Jesus in a central position. This is probably not historically accurate. When God commanded the Israelites to commemorate the Passover, he said that they were to eat standing up, as if they were about

✢

A stained-glass window, dating from 1842, which depicts the Last Supper (after Judas has left) at the church of St Leonard, Colchester.

to leave, in memory of the rushed last meal before the Exodus. However, by Roman times, reclining during meals was the mark of a free man, and so was considered more appropriate for a festival that celebrated freedom. The very earliest representations of the scene have Jesus and the apostles in reclining positions, with Jesus at the right of the table, the Roman position of honour.

Jesus may be taking the bread to break it, or blessing the cup of wine, or dipping into a bowl with Judas. Sitting next to Jesus is St John, beardless and with his head resting on Jesus' chest (some artists misinterpreted John's reclining position and portray him fast asleep!). Often no real attempt is made to distinguish the other disciples, but some or all of the following features can be used. PETER may sit near Jesus, in reference to his seniority. He has short curly grey hair and a beard, and is sometimes holding a knife, perhaps in a reference to his cutting off the ear of the slave of the High Priest, during THE BETRAYAL; ANDREW is usually more elderly, with flowing grey hair and a forked beard; JAMES THE GREAT and JAMES THE LESS were said to be brothers of Jesus, so can be portrayed with similar features and hairstyle to that worn by Jesus (James the Great will be sitting closer to Jesus, since he was the closer companion of the two); PHILIP and THOMAS are the youngest of the group, and may be clean-shaven; SIMON and JUDE were traditionally brothers, and are older and sitting together; BARTHOLOMEW and MATTHEW may both have dark hair and beards.

The treacherous Judas Iscariot often sits slightly apart from the group, or else is already up and leaving the room to betray Jesus. Since he was the money-holder for the group, he is usually carrying or wearing a purse, a device that also alludes to the thirty pieces of silver he accepted to betray Jesus. Unlike the other apostles, he may have been denied a HALO – or been given one that is black. Judas may also have his back to the viewer, or be shown side-on. In Byzantine artistic tradition, evil persons could not be portrayed looking outwards, because if an onlooker caught their gaze it might corrupt them. The tradition seems to have been followed in Western art.

✣

Detail of a stained-glass window depicting Jesus at the Last Supper, at the church of St Catherine, Boot, Eskdale, Cumbria.

Jesus Washes the Feet of the Disciples

During THE LAST SUPPER, Jesus poured water into a basin and began to wash his disciples' feet, drying them with the towel that was wrapped around his waist. When he came to wash ST PETER'S feet, Peter resisted. Jesus explained that he was setting an example that they should do as he had done. No servant, he said, was greater than his master, nor is a messenger greater than the one who sent him (John 13:1–17). It is always Peter's feet – with Peter looking rather uncomfortable, or with a hand raised in protest – that Jesus is shown washing.

The Agony in the Garden

The word 'Agony' comes from the Greek word *agon*, a contest. It is a reference to the turmoil of mind that Jesus went through before giving himself up to betrayal and CRUCIFIXION, the contest between his wish to avoid the suffering to come and his obedience to God, or a conflict between his human and divine natures. After THE LAST SUPPER, Jesus went with his disciples to the Garden of Gethsemane. He took ST PETER, ST JOHN, and ST JAMES THE GREAT with him as he went further into the garden to pray. The three disciples fell asleep and Jesus woke them (saying to Peter, 'The spirit is willing, but the body is weak'), and twice more returned to prayer, only to find them asleep again. In one version of LUKE'S account, an angel appeared to strengthen Jesus, and he prayed so earnestly that 'his sweat became like great drops of blood falling down on the ground' (Luke 22:43–44). The vivid images of the strengthening ANGEL and the sweat like blood are often reproduced.

The night-time scene includes Jesus praying, often kneeling on a rocky outcrop, with the three sleeping disciples below.

✢

A carving on a reredos at the church of St Edmund, Southwold, Suffolk, showing Jesus washing the feet of St Peter. The disciples to the rear look distinctly uncomfortable.

THE BETRAYAL

JUDAS then arrived at the garden with a detachment of soldiers and officials, carrying torches, swords, and clubs. He identified Jesus to the soldiers by kissing him, and this 'Judas kiss' can form the focus of the scene. John's Gospel does not mention the kiss, but says that when Jesus identified himself the soldiers fell to the ground. These two elements – the kiss and the collapsing soldiers – are sometimes combined into the one scene.

PETER drew his sword and struck off the right ear of Malchus, the slave of the High Priest. Jesus told Peter to put his sword back in its sheath, and he touched and healed Malchus' ear, showing compassion and forgiveness, even at this heightened moment (Luke 22:39–53 and John 18:1–11). The disciples took to their heels, and are sometimes shown running away. An odd detail from Mark's Gospel may also be included. A young man was following the disciples dressed only in a linen cloth. The soldiers tried to grab him, but he slipped out of the cloth and ran away naked (Mark 14:51–52). The young man has traditionally been identified as MARK himself.

THE TRIALS OF JESUS

The Gospels have various accounts of THE TRIALS OF JESUS, including before Caiphas (the Jewish High Priest; Matthew 26:57–68), Annas (Caiphas' father-in-law; John 18:12–23), Herod (tetrarch of Galilee, representing the civil authorities; Luke 23:8–12), and Pontius Pilate (the Roman governor; Luke 23:13–25).

Jesus was accused of blasphemy and condemned by Caiphas/Annas and the Jewish authorities. They needed the approval of the authorities before he could be executed, so Jesus was taken before Pontius Pilate. Pilate said that he could find no basis for any accusation against him, and sent him to Herod, who, confronted by Jesus' silence, sent him back again.

Pilate's wife had sent him a message that he should have nothing to do with the condemnation of Jesus, and scenes can show her messenger speaking in Pilate's ear. It was the custom at the feast of Passover to release a prisoner, and Pilate offered the crowd the choice of releasing Jesus or Barabbas, a man who had been condemned for insurrection and murder. The crowd cried out for Jesus to be crucified, in spite of Pilate continuing to protest his innocence. Pilate then washed his hands before the crowd, saying that he would be innocent of this man's blood, before he allowed the execution to proceed.

THE FLAGELLATION

As was the usual practice before crucifixion, Jesus was flogged. Although THE FLAGELLATION is only mentioned in passing in the Gospels, harrowing medieval accounts of visions of the event made representations popular. The mystic Margery Kempe had a vision of sixteen men with sixteen lead-tipped scourges giving Jesus forty blows each. The scene is sometimes set in Pilate's house, and shows Jesus tied to a narrow post or pillar.

✥

Judas brings the soldiers, carrying lanterns, swords and clubs, to the garden and betrays Jesus with a kiss.

The Crowning
with Thorns

After THE FLAGELLATION, a whole cohort of soldiers gathered around Jesus in Pilate's headquarters. They stripped him, put a scarlet (or purple) robe around his shoulders, a twisted CROWN OF THORNS on his head, and a reed in his hand (in imitation of a sceptre), then knelt before him saying, 'Hail, King of the Jews!' They spat on him and beat him, before dressing him in his own clothes and leading him away to be crucified (Matthew 27:27–31). The scene can include elements from the earlier Mocking of Jesus (Matthew 26:67), which took place before his trial, when he was blindfolded and beaten with fists. The two scenes can be distinguished because the Crowning was undertaken by soldiers, whereas the Mocking was by the people.

The Road to Calvary

Jesus was forced to carry his own cross, or at least the cross-beam, to the execution site. On the way, a man called Simon of Cyrene was forced to carry the cross for part of the way. Jesus also spoke to the women of Jerusalem, who were crying for him. He urged them not to cry for him but for themselves (this has been taken to be a prophecy of the brutal sacking of Jerusalem by Rome, which was to take place a few decades later). These scenes are set out more fully in the section on the STATIONS OF THE CROSS (page 67).

(page 67)

✣

Jesus wearing the Crown of Thorns. Kirchbach Roman Catholic Cemetery, Kärnten, Austria.

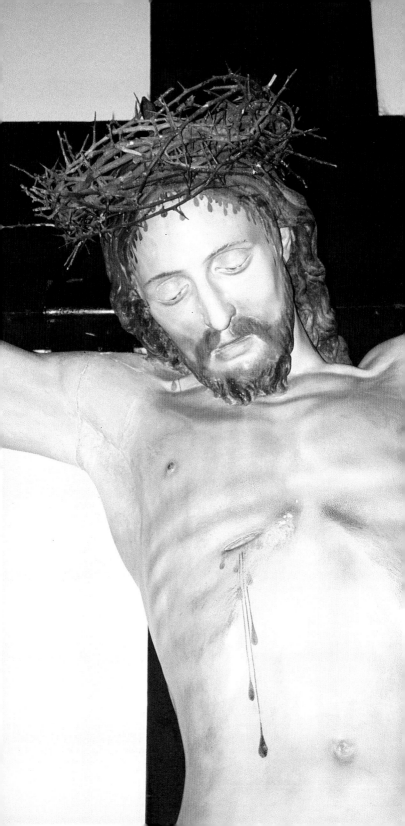

The Crucifixion

Jesus was crucified outside the walls of Jerusalem at a site called Golgotha (in Greek, Calvary), which means 'Place of the Skull'. In reference to the name, images often include a skull or skulls around the base of the cross. The site's name may be a reference to its function as an execution-ground, or there may have been something skull-like about it: one of the sites in present-day Jerusalem that is claimed to be Golgotha lies beside a rocky outcrop that resembles a skull.

In images of THE CRUCIFIXION, the skull can also be a reference to the grave of Adam. Theologians came to see Jesus as the 'New Adam', whose crucifixion bridged the division between humankind and God that Adam had caused (see THE FALL/ADAM AND EVE, page 262). In theological terms, the skull in this context was Jesus laying to rest the sin of Adam, but in addition, legends developed that explicitly connected Jesus and Adam. One of these was that Golgotha lay on the site of Adam's grave – so it is Adam's skull that is represented.

Jesus was stripped of his clothes and nailed to the Cross. Above him, Pilate had fixed the sign 'Jesus of Nazareth, King of the Jews'. His garment was 'without seam, woven in one piece', and so rather than cut it the Roman soldiers gambled for it (pictures have them throwing dice, and sometimes fighting among themselves). The crowds below mocked Jesus, telling him to save himself if he was God's chosen one.

Two criminals were crucified at the same time on either side of Jesus. MATTHEW and MARK record that they cursed Jesus with the crowd, but LUKE records that one of them rebuked the other and asked Jesus to remember him, to which Jesus replied, 'I tell you the truth, today you will be with me in paradise.' The thieves became known as Dismas and Gestas. Dismas the good is on Jesus' right-hand (good) side. He is sometimes the younger of the two, and may have a serene expression, looking towards Jesus as his soul is carried away by angels; Gestas is older, twisted with hate and pain, and as he

✛

Detail of a typical example of a Crucifix. Jesus' head, still wearing the crown of thorns, hangs to the right, while his side has been pierced by the Roman soldier's spear.

looks away from Jesus his soul may be being dragged downwards by demons. Two further points. First, the crosses of the criminals are usually smaller than Jesus', in accordance with the artistic convention that greater size meant greater honour. Secondly, in Western art they are sometimes tied, not nailed, to their crosses.

ST JOHN is named as having been present at the Crucifixion, as were THE VIRGIN MARY and ST MARY MAGDALENE, and they are usually shown at the base of the Cross. From the Cross, Jesus gave his mother and John into one another's care. Darkness then came across the land. In some medieval and early Renaissance pictures the sun and the moon appear, with the sun on Jesus' right and the moon on his left, occasionally with human faces and veiled with cross-hatching, or part-covered by a cloud. They also show the two natures of Jesus, the sun representing his divinity and the moon his humanity, or the New and Old Testaments, since the Old Testament (the moon) was thought by St Augustine to be simply a reflection of the light shed by the New Testament (the sun).

Jesus cried out in Aramaic, '*Eloi, Eloi, lema sabachthani?*' meaning 'My God, my God, why have you forsaken me?' One of those present (traditionally named Stephanon) dipped hyssop in vinegar (or sour wine, the alcohol being intended to ease the agony), placed it on a reed, and raised it for Jesus to drink. With a final cry, Jesus died.

A soldier pierced his side with a spear, and a mixture of blood and water flowed out. This outpouring was interpreted as symbolizing two of the sacraments, BAPTISM (water) and THE EUCHARIST (blood), and with this in mind sometimes an angel is portrayed catching the flow of blood from Jesus' side in a communion chalice. The soldier has been given the name Longinus, which means 'lance'. In one story he was blind until Jesus' blood fell into his eyes and cured him, and so sometimes he is pointing to his eyes, or else someone is shown guiding his hand with the lance. Additional allegorical details can include a PELICAN at the top of the Cross, and, in the Middle Ages, figures representing the Church and the Synagogue.

⁜

St Mary Magdalene, with long, flowing hair at the base of the Cross during the Crucifixion. Detail from a stained-glass window at the church of St Mary, Culworth, Hampshire.

THE DESCENT FROM THE CROSS AND THE PIETA

In THE DESCENT FROM THE CROSS, or 'the Deposition', Jesus' blood-streaked body is brought down from the Cross, as ST JOHN, THE VIRGIN MARY, and ST MARY MAGDALENE look on. Joseph of Arimathea, a Jewish council member, and a lawyer called Nicodemus (who had appeared previously in the Gospels, asking Jesus questions and defending him to the Pharisees, John 3:1–21 & 7:50–52) may also be present: in the apocryphal Gospel of Nicodemus, Joseph was said to have supported Jesus' body while Nicodemus drew out the nails. Joseph and Nicodemus appear together in the Gospels in the Entombment. Joseph asked to be given the body of Jesus. Together, he and Nicodemus wrapped Jesus' body in a clean linen cloth with spices, then placed it in Joseph's own tomb, hewn out of the rock. A stone was rolled over the entrance to seal the tomb (Matthew 27:57–61; Mark 15:42–47; Luke 23:50–56; John 19:38–42).

✥

The Virgin Mary and St John lamenting over the Crucified Jesus after the Descent from the Cross.
Above, *The dead body of Jesus is brought down from the cross.*

The moment of RESURRECTION is not recorded in the Gospels, but is widely portrayed in the art of the Western Church. Jesus emerges in glory from the tomb. He is dressed in white or gold and may be holding the banner of the Resurrection, a pole bearing a pendant with a red cross on a white background. Jesus' wounds are visible, to confirm that he is the Jesus who died, and to glorify the suffering that he endured.

The type of tomb portrayed varied over time. Often Jesus was shown stepping out of the sort of modern box-tomb that would have been familiar to the artist and viewers. In sixteenth century depictions, Jesus tends to stand before a closed tomb, after the Roman Catholic Church condemned the scriptural inaccuracy of portraying him emerging from it.

The Gospel accounts of the discovery of the Resurrection differ slightly. According to MATTHEW, MARK and LUKE, in the early morning, MARY MAGDALENE and other women came to the tomb with spices to anoint Jesus' body. They found that the stone had been rolled away from the entrance. A man or two men dressed in bright white clothes (presumably ANGELS) told them that Jesus had risen. According to Matthew, Jesus himself then appeared to the women, and told them to tell the other disciples what they had seen. In JOHN'S account, Mary Magdalene found the tomb empty. She told PETER and John, who found the linen wrappings lying alone in the tomb. They returned home, while Mary Magdalene remained, where she encountered the two angels and then the risen Jesus in person.

Roman soldiers are often shown slumped around the tomb. Matthew's Gospel records that the Pharisees were worried that the disciples would steal Jesus' body and then claim that he had risen from the dead. Pilate therefore gave permission to station a guard of soldiers at the tomb. When an angel appeared and rolled back the stone, the guards 'shook and became like dead things'. Over time, the guards came to be portrayed sleeping (Matthew 28:1–10).

✠

The Resurrection of Christ. Detail from a stained-glass window at the church of St Leonard, Colchester, Essex. There are scars on Jesus' hands and in his side.

THE INCREDULITY OF
THOMAS

THOMAS was not present when Jesus appeared to the disciples. They told him that Jesus had returned, but he declared that he would not believe it unless he put his fingers in the nail-marks in Jesus' hands, and his hand in the wound in Jesus' side. A week later, Jesus appeared to them in a locked room, and invited Thomas to touch his hands and side. Thomas responded, 'My Lord and my God!' (John 20:24–29).

Thomas' flood of belief came after he was invited to touch the wounds, and in art he is often shown in contact with the wounds. The scene is sometimes represented in a stylized way, with a hand reaching into the crack of a broken heart.

THE ASCENSION

Forty days after THE RESURRECTION, Jesus led the disciples to Bethany. He raised his hands, blessed them, and then was lifted up until a cloud took him out of their sight. As the disciples were gazing upwards, two ANGELS appeared with them, dressed in white. They said that Jesus would return to them in the same way as they had seen him leave (Luke 24:50 and Acts 1:9–11).

In the Church of the Ascension on the Mount of Olives there is an indentation in the rock that is meant to be Jesus' last footprint on earth. This hole in the rock is sometimes included in images of THE ASCENSION. Eleven apostles look on (they had not yet replaced Judas), accompanied by THE VIRGIN MARY. In the earliest portrayals, Jesus steps up to reach the hand of God, or rises upwards supported by angels. In Eastern art, Jesus had to be portrayed in full frontal; in the West, it is more usual to see him in profile, as if climbing to heaven, or disappearing into a cloud, with his feet and the hem of his clothes visible.

✣

Jesus ascends to heaven, surrounded by an aureole, and watched by the Virgin Mary and disciples. The Ascension is particularly revered by the Eastern Church.

PENTECOST, when THE HOLY SPIRIT filled the disciples, followed THE ASCENSION. It is considered to be the birth of the Church, and is one of its major feasts.

The disciples were all together in a house, when it was filled with a sound like a rushing wind. Tongues of fire appeared and touched each one of them, and they began to speak in other languages. A crowd gathered at the noise: some were amazed, while others sneered and accused the disciples of being drunk. ST PETER responded that they could not be drunk since it was only nine o'clock in the morning, and started preaching about Jesus (Acts 2).

The Holy Spirit is represented by the tongues of fire themselves, and also as a DOVE hovering above the scene. The biblical account of Pentecost does not state that THE VIRGIN MARY was present, but it does say that she and the disciples were constantly at prayer together, and she is usually included and even placed at the centre of the scene: at the birth of the Church, she represents the Church itself. The words *Effundam de Spiritu meo super omnem carnem* (Latin: 'I will pour out my spirit on all flesh') can appear near the scene. These were words that Peter spoke to the gathering crowd, and are a quotation from the Prophet Joel (2:28).

In Eastern and some Renaissance art, a man appears with twelve scrolls, or twelve figures appear in various form of dress. The scrolls represent the languages of the world that the disciples were speaking, and the people are the people of the world to whom they were speaking.

✛

Tongues of fire touch the heads of the disciples at Pentecost and (above) The Holy Spirit, with cruciform halo and in the form of a dove, descends from heaven to earth.

THE LAST JUDGEMENT

(DOOM)

In Matthew's Gospel, Jesus said that he would sit in judgement on the world, separating the people like a shepherd separates SHEEP from GOATS. The righteous, who had fed the hungry and given the thirsty something to drink, welcomed strangers, clothed the naked, cared for the sick, and visited prisoners, would inherit the kingdom of God; the damned, who had not done these things, would go to eternal fire (Matthew 25:31–46).

This has become known as THE LAST JUDGEMENT, or THE DOOM. Jesus sits in glory with his wounds visible and may be portrayed with a sword emerging from his mouth, a golden sash across his chest, and seven stars in his right hand, following the description of him in ST JOHN'S vision in Revelation (1:16). The dead rise up from their graves. On Jesus' right, the saved enter heaven; on his left, the damned are dragged by demons into hell.

Heaven can appear as a fortified city, or a garden, and ST PETER may be welcoming the souls of the saved. Heaven can also be symbolized by a looped cloth held by an old man. The old man is ABRAHAM, and the image comes from one of the parables of Jesus, in which Dives, a rich man, ignored Lazarus, a poor man who was starving at his gate. Lazarus went to heaven and Dives to hell, from where he could see Lazarus 'in Abraham's bosom'. 'Bosom' (*sinus*) could also be translated as the fold at the neck of a toga, used as a pocket – hence the looped cloth (Luke 16:19–31). Hell is usually cavernous and sometimes the mouth of a monster, in a reference to LEVIATHAN.

Doom paintings are often loaded with symbolism. A pair of scales held by an ANGEL (it is the ARCHANGEL MICHAEL) is the weighing of souls, righteous souls generally being the heavier (the devil or a demon may be trying to skew the balance by tipping one side of the scales towards damnation, while THE VIRGIN MARY tips the other side towards mercy); an angel (traditionally the ARCHANGEL GABRIEL) or angels may be blowing trumpets, from the account of the seven angels ushering the Second Coming of the Messiah in the Book of Revelation (8:7 – 11:19), and Jesus' words, that in the last days 'he will send out his angels with a loud trumpet call' (Matthew 24:31); a tree

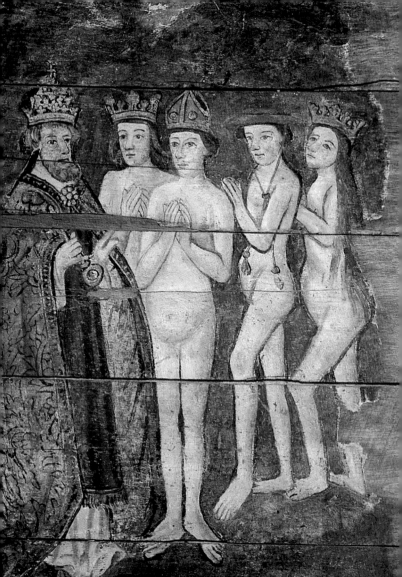

Detail of a wall painting at the church of St Peter, Wenhaston, Suffolk, depicting The Last Judgement. Bishops, cardinals, kings and queens, all of them naked in death, are nervously approaching St Peter, who holds the keys of heaven.

❖

entwined with a SNAKE is the Tree of the Knowledge of Good and Evil; a ladder symbolizes the cross, by which man can ascend to heaven. Specific sins can also be represented, for example a miser with his money bags.

189

Representations of The Virgin Mary

Christians revere THE VIRGIN MARY because she is the Mother of Jesus, and therefore the Mother of God. She is honoured as a model of obedience and faithfulness, while her sufferings as a mother add to the empathy that many feel with her. In her hymn of praise and joy after THE ANNUNCIATION (Luke 1:46–55; see page 199) she says that 'from henceforth all generations shall call me blessed'. This has led to the title that honours her before all other saints – the Blessed Virgin Mary.

Mary has been the subject of sharp theological divisions between Roman Catholic and Protestant Churches, and when iconoclasts destroyed images in churches they fell on images of Mary with particular fury. Protestants objected to the level of veneration accorded to her, which they felt seemed at times to be as great as that given to Jesus. They also objected to some of the doctrines that the Roman Catholic Church allowed to Mary: that she was without sin, that she remained a virgin throughout her life, and that she was physically assumed into heaven at her death. These teachings seemed to Protestants to be without biblical authority, and to elevate Mary to a position that was more than mortal. In more recent times, though, it is probably fair to say that there has been a

✣

Bernardino Fungal (1460–1516), The Holy Family, *an Italian artist of the Sienese School. and* (above) *a statue of the Virgin Mary and Jesus at the church of St Mary, Broxted, Essex.*

softening of approach and appreciation of Mary among many Protestant Churches.

Mary is almost always portrayed dressed in blue. The colour blue was at one time the most expensive in an artist's repertoire, and so was used sparingly and only on the most precious objects. Mary's chief attribute of a white LILY expresses her purity and virginity,

The Fleur-de-Lys

The Pierced Heart

and may have originated from representations of the Annunciation, which traditionally took place in the flower-filled springtime. The lily is sometimes expressed heraldically as a fleur-de-lys (also a symbol of THE TRINITY). She is also represented by a ROSE, the most beautiful of flowers. Again, the rose is often portrayed in a stylized, heraldic form.

Other ways of representing Mary symbolically include a heart pierced with a sword, often with wings (see SACRED HEART, page 146); and the letter M, alone or as part of a sacred monogram (see LETTERS AND WORDS, page 129).

A common image of Mary is standing alone on a crescent moon, shining in glory and with an array of twelve stars around her head. This comes from the Book of Revelation, which talks

Sacred Monogram

of 'a woman clothed with the sun', commonly identified as Mary. The passage is mystical, mysterious, and terrifying: 'A great and wondrous sign appeared in heaven: a woman clothed with the sun, with the moon under her feet and a crown of twelve stars on her head. She was pregnant and cried out in pain as she was about to give birth. Then another sign appeared in heaven: an enormous red DRAGON with seven heads and ten horns and seven crowns on his heads. His tail swept a third of the stars out of the sky and flung them to the earth. The dragon stood in front of the woman who was about to give birth, so that he might devour her child the moment it was born. She gave birth to a son, a male child, who will rule all the nations with an iron sceptre. And her child was snatched up to God and to his throne' (Revelation 12:1–5).

*Madonna and Child, depicted in a mass-produced icon of the
Eastern Church.*

✛ JOACHIM & ANNE/ANNA

MARY'S parents were called JOACHIM AND ANNE, or ANNA. No mention is made of them in the Bible, but stories about them were told in the apocryphal Gospel of James, which dates from the second century.

The couple had been childless for many years. Joachim was humiliated when he brought a LAMB to the Temple, which the High Priests refused to allow him to sacrifice because he had not fathered a child. Ashamed, he did not return home, but instead went to stay with shepherds in the desert. There, the ANGEL GABRIEL appeared to him and foretold that Anne would conceive, and that he should go to meet her by the Golden Gate in Jerusalem (images of the appearance have the angel and Joachim with SHEEP or shepherds nearby). Anne, who had received the same angelic message, was waiting under a LAUREL tree by the Golden Gate. She looked up at a nest of sparrows in the tree, and lamented that, unlike her, even the birds of the air were fruitful. Joachim met her and kissed her, and it was the convention that at that moment she became pregnant. The Golden Gate, which faces onto the Temple Mount in Jerusalem, is walled shut. It appears in the tender scene of the reuniting of Joachim and Anne in gold or topped with gold, while its closed arch represents Mary's virginity.

✛

Wooden statues of the Virgin Mary as a child and her mother Anne, at the church of Santa Fosca, Torcello, near Venice, Italy.

✣ THE NATIVITY OF MARY

Representations of the birth of MARY are within a well-appointed house (JOACHIM was a wealthy man), or sometimes in a church, since Mary would be brought up in the Temple. ANNE may be reclining on a bed with midwives, the elderly Joachim may be nearby, with neighbours arriving with gifts.

✣ THE PRESENTATION

ANNE had prayed that if she could be blessed with a child, she would dedicate it to God's service. Therefore, when MARY was three, her parents took her to be presented at the Temple. She climbed the fifteen steps to the Temple as if she was older than her years, and then danced before the altar. She was left in the Temple with the other virgins, where she spun wool and embroidered clothes for the priests.

✣ THE MARRIAGE

When MARY was fourteen, an ANGEL visited the High Priest to tell him to arrange a husband for her. The angel said that men of marriageable age should be assembled, with their staffs. JOSEPH, a carpenter from Nazareth, was among them. He was shown to be the husband chosen by God when his staff blossomed; an alternative legend has a DOVE landing on it. The flowering rod was thought to represent Mary, since it flowered without being fertilized. In the marriage scene, the couple are shown before the High Priest, Joseph holding his sprouting or dove-topped staff, and placing a ring on Mary's finger.

✣

Stained-glass window showing Mary at the Temple,
at St Leonard's Church,
Colchester, Essex.

REPRESENTATIONS OF THE VIRGIN MARY

196

The Annunciation

The first event in MARY's life told in the Bible is ST LUKE's account of THE ANNUNCIATION. The Annunciation is a simple and very common scene, due to the importance of the Church's teaching on the conception of Jesus, and the many religious and lay groups that took the event as their patronage.

The ANGEL GABRIEL appeared to Mary in Nazareth, with the words 'Greetings, favoured one, the Lord is with you' (which may be written *Ave, gratia plena, Dominus tecum*, or simply *Ave Maria*). He told her that she would conceive through the power of THE HOLY SPIRIT, and bear a son to be called Jesus, who would be a mighty ruler. In the face of this alarming announcement, Mary responded faithfully and obediently: 'Behold the handmaiden of the Lord, let it be to me according to your will' (*Ecce ancilla Domini, fiat mihi secundum verbum tuum*; Luke 1:26–38). The conception and incarnation of Jesus is believed to have taken place at this moment of submission, and is the moment portrayed. The festival of the Annunciation is held on 25 March, exactly nine months before the birth of Jesus is celebrated.

The key elements in the scene are Mary, the Angel Gabriel (carrying a sceptre or LILY), and the Holy Spirit descending on Mary in the form of a DOVE. As the Annunciation was held to have taken place in springtime, it is often in or beside a flowering garden, or else flowers (usually lilies) are shown in a vase. Mary may be reading a book, on which are written the prophetic words of ISAIAH, *Ecce virgo concipiet et pariet filium* ('Behold, the Virgin will conceive and will give birth to a son'; Isaiah 7:14). Close to Mary may be wool or fabrics, in a reference to her work on the High Priest's clothes when she lived in the Temple.

✣

The Annunciation: the Angel Gabriel, carrying his and Mary's attribute of a lily, appears to Mary, while the Holy Spirit descends in the form of a dove. Stained-glass window at the church of St Mary and St Peter, Weedon Lois, Northamptonshire.

JOSEPH'S DREAM

JOSEPH was very disturbed when he discovered that MARY was pregnant, and he planned to end their engagement quietly. However, an ANGEL appeared to him in a dream and explained that the child was from THE HOLY SPIRIT, and would fulfil ISAIAH'S prophecy (Matthew 1:18–25). Joseph may be portrayed slumbering at his carpenter's bench, surrounded by his tools, as THE ANGEL GABRIEL appears overhead.

THE VISITATION

After THE ANNUNCIATION, MARY went to visit her relative Elizabeth, who was pregnant with ST JOHN THE BAPTIST. When Mary approached, Elizabeth cried out: 'Blessed are you among women and blessed is the fruit of your womb!' (*Benedicta tu inter mulieres et benedictus fructus ventris tui*). John leaped for joy in the womb of his mother (Luke 1:39–56).

Elizabeth was barren and elderly (by the standards of the time) when she conceived John, and was six months pregnant at THE VISITATION, and so there should be a contrast between her older appearance and heavier pregnancy and Mary's youth and smaller bump. The women's husbands may hover in the background, Joseph in his worker's clothes and Zechariah in priestly robes. This meeting between the two women gave atists licence to sometimes include John with Jesus as infants at play together.

THE ANNUNCIATION OF MARY'S DEATH

From the cross, Jesus had given MARY and ST JOHN to one another as mother and son, and so Mary joined John's household (John 19:26–27). After the Gospel accounts, Mary may have travelled to Ephesus in Ancient Greece (now Turkey), although in another tradition she died in Jerusalem.

Desperately lonely, Mary would visit the sites of events in her son's life (including THE STATIONS OF THE CROSS in Jerusalem), but longed to be with him again. An ANGEL appeared to her and foretold that in three days' time she would die and be reunited with her son in Paradise. The angel gave her a PALM BRANCH, which she gave to St John to carry before her at burial. Portrayals of the scene are similar to THE ANNUNCIATION, except that Mary is portrayed as an older woman and the angel carries a palm instead of a sceptre or LILY.

THE DEATH OF MARY

MARY had asked the angel that all of the apostles should be present at her death, and they therefore all appear grouped around her bed. ST PETER is usually at the head of the bed, conducting the service, while ST JOHN is at the foot, holding the PALM that Mary had given him. ST THOMAS may be just coming in through the door, late because he has had to come all the way from evangelizing in India. Suddenly, the room was filled with light, and Jesus appeared to take his mother's soul to heaven. In a touching reversal of the familiar image of the Madonna and child, Jesus is sometimes shown cradling the soul of his mother. In one tradition, Mary did not die before THE ASSUMPTION, and so the event is sometimes called the Dormition (Falling Asleep).

✛

Mary and Elizabeth meet at The Visitation. Mary is on the more honoured right-hand side and the depiction of her hair (in contrast to Elizabeth's full covering) signifies her comparative youth.

MAGNA MATER DEI

ORA PRO NOBIS

The Funeral Procession & Entombment

Occasionally, THE FUNERAL PROCESSION AND ENTOMBMENT of MARY are shown. In one legend, the High Priest tried to stop the funeral by pushing at the bier. His hands stuck and he was released only when he agreed that Jesus was the Messiah.

The Assumption

In the teaching of the Roman Catholic and Eastern Churches, three days after her death, MARY'S soul was reunited with her body, and both were assumed into heaven. The Death and ASSUMPTION of Mary forms a small cycle of its own. Again, the stories do not appear in the Bible, but are derived from apocrypha and traditional stories. Scenes have Mary rising from her tomb, attended by ANGELS, while the disciples look on. Knowing ST THOMAS' reputation for scepticism, she may be dropping her girdle (belt) to him, as proof of her passing.

The Coronation of the Virgin

The CORONATION OF MARY (the final part of the Dormition cycle), shows MARY richly robed and surrounded by ANGELS, being crowned Queen of Heaven by her son, often sitting at his right hand. Sometimes all three persons of THE TRINITY crown her, GOD THE FATHER and GOD THE SON holding the crown while THE HOLY SPIRIT hovers above in the form of a DOVE.

✛

A plaque of Our Lady Assumed into Heaven, at St Columba's Cathedral, Oban, Scotland.

Recognising Saints & Angels 8

Saints

There are two Hebrew words in the Bible that translate as the English 'saint'. One simply refers to pious, godly people (for example, Psalm 30:4); the other indicates people who are holy, and separated to God (for example, Psalm 16:3). The latter is the meaning used in the New Testament, where for the most part it is used to describe the Christian faithful (for example, Romans 1:7). In this meaning, everyone who confesses to the Christian faith is a saint.

In the context of church imagery, saints are particularly holy men and women, recognized as such by the Church. The power to 'declare' sainthood derives from Jesus' commission to ST PETER: 'I will give you the keys of the kingdom of heaven; whatever you bind on earth will be bound in heaven, and whatever you loose on earth will be loosed in heaven' (Matthew 16:18). Over the centuries, the choice of person to be sainted has been influenced in varying parts by genuine devotion, fashion, and politics, to produce a mixed bag of saints, from the largely made-up to the truly inspirational.

✤

Stained glass window depicting St Peter, and (above) *saints on a rood screen: (left to right) Simon, Andrew and Peter.*

Saints have an ancient role as 'intercessors' between God and man. Since God could seem too awesome to be approachable, the prayerful could ask the saints in heaven to intercede for them with God. They are therefore not, as such, prayed to, they are simply asked to pray *to* God on behalf of the praying person. Children's names were often taken from saints, originally in the hope that the namesake saint would then watch over the child and include him or her in their prayers.

Church names were also taken from saints, a tradition that began when the church would be named after the saint whose relics it held. The saint in question will have a particular association with the church named, and the church will most likely have a higher than usual number of references to that saint within its walls. The saint is meant to watch over that church, and the church generally returns the compliment by holding a special celebration on the saint's feast day.

There are a multitude of saints, and a multitude of books about them. The most common are those that appear in the Bible, and in this section we deal with those and a few of the most popular post-biblical saints.

✢

The stained-glass window at St German's Church, Cornwall, designed by William Morris (1834–96). Depicted are: (from top left) Longinus (the centurion who pierced the side of Jesus), St Mary Magdalene, Jesus, the Virgin Mary, and St Paul; (from bottom left) St Matthew, St Mark, St Stephen, St Luke, and St John. Above, *After the Resurrection, some of the disciples were fishing on the Sea of Tiberius when Jesus appeared on the beach. To reach the shore quicker, St Peter jumped into the lake.*

St John the Baptist

JOHN THE BAPTIST is easily recognizable by his wild dress, ragged hair and beard: he was a wild, ascetic holy man, preaching repentance in the Judaean desert, dressed in clothes of camel's hair and a leather belt, and living on a diet of locusts and wild honey. John baptized in the River Jordan those who heard his message and turned back to God. The first to describe Jesus as the 'LAMB OF GOD' he is sometimes depicted standing beside, or carrying, a LAMB. The long thin cross he carries symbolizes the long staff of a preacher or missionary.

John and Jesus were related, as their mothers Elizabeth and Mary are described by LUKE as kinsfolk. Elizabeth had no children and was getting on in years, as was her husband, Zechariah, to whom the ANGEL GABRIEL appeared with the news that he would have a son called John, who would be a great holy man – a forerunner of THE ANNUNCIATION. Zechariah did not believe the angel, and so was struck dumb only regaining his speech after his son was born. Mary and Elizabeth met in THE VISITATION (page 200), when they were both pregnant. This meeting gave artists licence to sometimes include John with Jesus as infants at play together.

John is seen as a forward messenger for Jesus, referred to by the Prophets ISAIAH and Malachi. He baptized Jesus, at the start of Jesus' ministry and died at the hands of King Herod. His uncompromising beliefs led him to rebuke Herod publicly for having married Herodias, the wife of his brother (John 14:1–12). As a result Herod had John imprisoned, although he showed no sign of wanting John dead, and used to visit him in prison. At a banquet, Herodias' daughter Salome danced for his guests and Herod was so impressed that he unwisely promised to give her anything she chose. Prompted by her mother, who was looking for revenge for John's rebuke, Salome asked that she be brought the head of John the Baptist on a platter. Images of this scene, in which the beautiful Salome is contrasted with John's gory head, were extremely popular.

⁜

Wooden carving of John the Baptist from the Church of the Holy Trinity, Blythburgh, Suffolk. An unusually serene John is shown holding the Lamb of God.

Joseph was husband of THE VIRGIN MARY, foster-father of Jesus, and protector of the Holy Family. Centuries of mockery and rough treatment of Joseph in popular art and medieval plays have given way to honour for his strength of character, devotion, and kindness. He was, as MATTHEW says, 'a just man' (Matthew 1:19). His strength of character is apparent in his first appearance in the Gospels. Matthew records that when Mary became pregnant, she was engaged to Joseph. Becoming engaged was treated at the time as marriage for the purpose of sexual relations, so that Mary's pregnancy would not have been a surprise to anyone – except to Joseph. Matthew makes it clear that Joseph did not want to expose Mary to public disgrace, but instead planned to end the engagement quietly. Before he could do so, an ANGEL appeared to Joseph in a dream and told him that the unborn child was from THE HOLY SPIRIT.

Joseph is often depicted as being an old man. He is not mentioned as having been present at Jesus' CRUCIFIXION, and is therefore supposed to have died before Jesus started his public life. In addition, apocryphal sources claim that he was an elderly widower when he married Mary (his children from his previous marriage being the brothers of Jesus referred to in the Gospels). Joseph sometimes has the attribute of a LILY. Traditionally, his staff sprouted to show that he was God's choice as a husband for Mary. The blossoming staff became the lily, as a reflection of the Virgin Mary's attribute of a lily, and as a symbol of Joseph's purity.

The fact of his fiancée falling pregnant, his supposed age, and the Catholic teaching that Mary remained a virgin throughout her life, caused Joseph to be an object of some derision, particularly in the Middle Ages. In paintings of THE NATIVITY, Joseph was sometimes given an 'embarrassing' role, such as washing nappies in the background, but he has been rehabilitated since these bawdier times through his qualities of kindness, strength and care in protecting Jesus.

✧

St Joseph depicted in a stained-glass window at
St Leonard's Church, Colchester, Essex, holding a lily to
signify his purity. The carpenter's square illustrates his profession.

✤ St Mary Magdalene

MARY MAGDALENE was a disciple of Jesus, and is one of the most vivid and appealing women in the Bible. With a troubled past, she was sensual, emotional, and completely devoted to Jesus, her devotion making her the subject of criticism from others. In images of her she is always beautiful, with long, often blonde or reddish hair. The name Magdalene may be a reference to Mary's home town of Magdala, or to an expression in the Talmud that means 'curling women's hair'.

Traditionally, Mary was a reformed prostitute. She is usually dressed in red to emphasize her love for Jesus, but also as a nod to her past as a 'scarlet woman'. In the Gospel accounts, she was possessed by seven demons, from which Jesus saved her (Luke 8:1). She followed Jesus from Galilee, stood at the foot of the cross, and is often present in scenes of THE CRUCIFIXION (Matthew 27:56). Above all, Christians honour Mary as the first person to whom Jesus revealed himself after THE RESURRECTION when he told her to go and inform the other disciples that he was alive (John 20:10–18).

Mary Magdalene's attribute is a jar or pot of perfume. Shortly before Jesus entered Jerusalem, a dinner was held in his honour at Mary's house. While her sister Martha served the guests, she took a jar of expensive perfume, poured it on Jesus' feet and wiped them with her long hair. JUDAS ISCARIOT rebuked her, on the grounds that the money for the perfume could better have been spent on the poor, but Jesus said that she was doing the proper thing, and was in fact preparing his body for death (John 12:1–8).

There are different traditions about Mary's life after the Gospel accounts. In the tradition of the Western Church, she went to France with Martha and her brother Lazarus, evangelized in Provence, became a hermit in the Maritime Alps, and died at Saint Maxime-La-Sainte-Baume. In the tradition of the Eastern Church, she went to Ephesus in Greece (now Turkey) with THE VIRGIN MARY and ST JOHN, where she died and was buried.

✣

A Crucifixion tableau, showing Mary Magdalene kneeling bare-headed, with her characteristic long hair, at the feet of Christ. The Virgin Mary kneels beside her and behind stands St John.

St Paul is called the Apostle to the Gentiles (whereas St Peter was the Apostle to the Jews; together they are known as the 'Princes of the Apostles'), and is regarded as the founder of the Church. He was not a disciple of Jesus and his conversion to become one of the Church's founding fathers is one of the most famous in history. His personality – opinionated, difficult, and passionate – emerges strongly through his letters in the New Testament. He is generally depicted with dark, receding hair and a pointed beard.

St Peter and St Paul

Paul was originally called Saul, and was born in the city of Tarsus in around AD 10. He was a Pharisee and a zealous persecutor of the early Church, hunting out Christians and 'breathing threats and murder against the disciples of the Lord' (Acts 9:1). He was present at the stoning to death of the first Christian martyr, St Stephen (Acts 7:58). But on the way to Damascus, Paul experienced a startling vision of Jesus. A great light flashed around him and he fell to the ground, from where he heard Jesus say: 'Saul, Saul, why do you persecute me?' Paul was struck blind, and Jesus told him to continue to Damascus. Jesus then appeared to a Christian in Damascus called Ananias, and told him to visit Paul and lay his hands on his eyes. Knowing Paul's reputation, Ananias was reluctant to go near him, but nevertheless obeyed Jesus' command. When Ananias laid his hands on him Paul regained his sight, and was baptized (Acts 9:1–19). Paul's preaching generated such hostility in Damascus that he had to escape through being lowered from the city walls in a basket. He travelled to Jerusalem, worked at Antioch, where he had a famous dispute with St Peter, and embarked on three great missionary journeys, to Cyprus, to Asia Minor, and to Macedonia and Achaea. Traditionally, Paul was executed in Rome during the persecutions of the Emperor Nero, on 29 June, the same day as St Peter. Whereas Peter was crucified, Paul was entitled as a Roman citizen to be executed by beheading with a sword (his major attribute).

✢

St Paul, St Leonard's Church, Bradford, West Yorkshire.

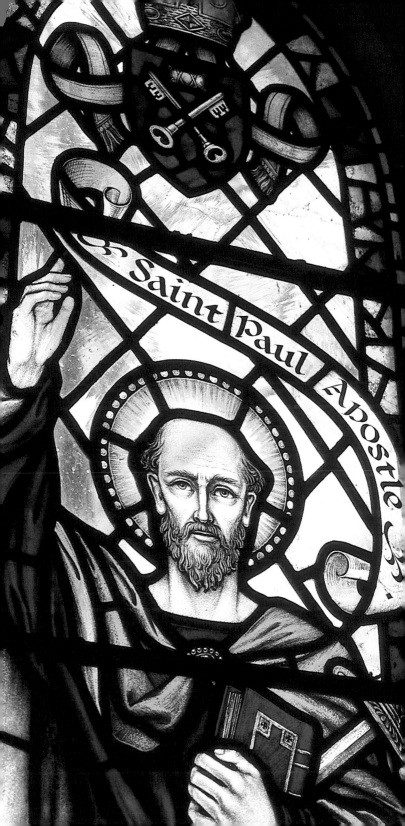
Saint Paul Apostle

*Carvings on the font at the church of St James, Nayland, Suffolk,
symbolizing Matthew, Mark, Luke, and John. Top left: the
angel is a symbol for St Matthew; Top right: the winged lion
represents St Mark; Bottom left: the winged bull for St Luke;
Bottom right: the eagle symbolizes St John.*

✛

The Four Evangelists

St matthew, st mark, st luke, and st john, each a writer of one of the four Gospels, are known as the four evangelists. Their symbols are, respectively, a man (or angel), a lion (often with wings), a bull or ox (likewise), and an eagle almost always found grouped together, for example at the four points of a cross, or in series on a panel. The symbols can be found either next to figures representing each of the Evangelists (so indicating which is which), or freestanding.

There are two sources for the symbols, both of them visionary. In the Old Testament, the Prophet ezekiel describes a vision of a divine chariot, ridden or driven by Cherubim (angels) each of which had 'four faces: one face was that of a cherub, the second the face of a man, the third the face of a lion, and the fourth the face of an eagle' (Ezekiel 1 & 10). In the New Testament, St John had a similar vision (Revelation 4:7–8). These visions were interpreted by Christian writers as representing the four Gospels, interconnected and moving together like the wheels in Ezekiel's vision, or together glorifying God like the creature in St John's vision.

Which of the four creatures was ascribed to which Evangelist depended on the nature of their Gospel. St Matthew was given the man/angel because his Gospel emphasizes Jesus' humanity. St Mark's Gospel was thought to emphasize Jesus' kingship, and so he was ascribed the lion, king of the beasts. His gospel also opens with St John's voice 'crying in the wilderness', like the roar of a lion. St Luke's bull is sacrificial, as he was thought to deal with the sacrificial aspects of Jesus' life, but also because his gospel begins with Zechariah, father of st john the baptist, making an offering to God. St John was ascribed the eagle because his Gospel is the most soaring and revelatory, and the eagle in mythology is the only bird able to look directly into the light of the sun. But the theme is one that attracts different interpretations. One commentator claimed that the four creatures appear around the cross because they are associated with the kingship of Jesus, in the centre, surrounded by man as the king of creation, the lion as king of wild animals, the ox as king of tame animals, and the eagle as king of the birds.

THE TWELVE APOSTLES

The Gospels name twelve disciples of Jesus. 'The Twelve' were picked by Jesus to be his companions and learn from him, but they also stood in an elevated position. They were given the power to exorcize demons, cure disease and infirmity, and ultimately to assist Jesus in judgement over humanity (Matthew 10:1 & 19:28, Luke 9:1 & 22:30).

But why only twelve when Jesus attracted thousands to hear him preach? The reason lies in the symbolism of the number. When God made his first covenant with Israel, Israel was divided into twelve tribes, although the system had become redundant by the time of Jesus. Now that a new covenant was being made through Jesus, the twelve disciples stood in place of these tribes. The 'thirteenth' apostle is St Matthias, chosen to replace the dead JUDAS ISCARIOT and maintain symbolic twelve.

In a church, the twelve can appear together, for example ranged in a tableau on either side of Jesus above the ALTAR, each identifiable by the symbol he holds, or by their physical appearance. They may be represented in a heraldic way, with their symbols set in shields, over the NAVE or in stained glass. They will appear in key scenes without their symbols, for example in THE LAST SUPPER, or as witnesses to a miracle, when it is often not possible to distinguish between them.

In a literary sense, the disciples as a group act as a chorus in the Gospels, asking the questions that elicit vital answers from Jesus, or standing dazed and baffled by Jesus' message or miracles. As individuals, some personalities – PETER, JOHN, and JAMES – emerge strongly, while others – JUDE, BARTHOLOMEW – remain permanently in the background. Similarly, while we have a reasonable idea of what happened to some of the apostles after the Gospel accounts of their lives, for others there remain only vague and unreliable traditions. They are, though, a hugely diverse and enjoyable group. Jesus put together a band of men that included the mystical and the sceptical, the boisterous and the timid, revolutionaries and traitors.

✥

St Matthew, church of St Andrew, Colton, Norfolk

PETER is a hugely popular saint, in part because of the strong, and very human, personality that emerges from the Gospels. He is impulsive and headstrong, at times almost comic, shown bald or tonsured, with a square face and rounded beard. Always first in lists of the disciples, Peter may have been their leader. He is considered to have been the first Pope and is shown dressed in bishop's robes or with a papal triple crown.

Originally called Simon, Peter was a fisherman and the brother of ST ANDREW. The brothers were fishing together when Jesus called them from the shore to follow him. We know that he was married, because Jesus healed his mother-in-law. When Jesus asked his disciples the key question, 'Who do you say I am?' it was Peter who said that he was the Messiah.

The accounts of Peter in the Gospels range from the absurd to the sublime, and from comedy to tragedy. When Jesus walked on water, Peter asked if he could do so too, only to start sinking (Matthew 14:22–32); when Jesus predicted his own death and Peter took him to one side to protest that this would never happen, Jesus berated him for diverting him from his mission ('Get behind me, Satan!', Matthew 16: 21–23).

Most famously, shortly before Jesus' arrest, when Peter said that he would never desert Jesus, Jesus predicted to Peter that that day he would deny knowing him three times before the COCK crowed at daybreak. During the night after Jesus' arrest, when asked by bystanders if he was one of Jesus' followers, Peter did indeed deny it three times, even going so far as to swear that he didn't know Jesus. When the cock crowed, and Peter realized what he had done, he wept bitterly. After Jesus' RESURRECTION, Peter was the first apostle to whom he appeared. In a reversal of the three denials, the risen Jesus asked Peter three times if he loved him, and when Peter answered that he did, charged him to 'tend my sheep', meaning his people. His most common attributes are keys, (the keys of heaven), a COCKEREL and an inverted cross, after the manner of his death by crucifixion.

✢

St Peter holding the keys of heaven depicted in a sixteenth-century stained-glass window at the church of St Mary the Virgin, Layer Marney, Essex.

JOHN was Jesus' favourite, his 'beloved disciple' (John 21:20). The Fourth Gospel, three epistles, and the Book of Revelation are attributed to him, although there is some question as to whether the same John wrote all of these. In churches, the beardless John is usually identifiable in two key events, THE LAST SUPPER (leaning against Jesus) and THE CRUCIFIXION (standing at the foot of the cross).

John was another fisherman, brother of ST JAMES THE GREAT. Both were passionate about Jesus' message and mission, and Jesus gave them the nickname Boanerges, 'sons of thunder' (Mark 3:17). When Jesus called them they were mending their fishing nets with their father Zebedee; they followed immediately, leaving their father with just the hired hands. They offered to call down fire from heaven when a village refused to welcome Jesus (for which they were rebuked by Jesus). The brothers are described in the Gospels as witnesses to THE TRANSFIGURATION and THE AGONY IN THE GARDEN.

After THE RESURRECTION and ASCENSION, John worked with ST PETER, to whom he was subordinate, and was imprisoned with him. Tradition has it that John was persecuted under the Emperor Domitian (including a miraculous escape from a cauldron of boiling oil), but lived to an old age in Ephesus.

The common image of John holding a chalice over which hangs a SERPENT (or a DRAGON) comes from a legend that he was challenged by a high priest of the goddess Diana at Ephesus to drink a cup of poison. He drank; not only was he unharmed, but he restored to life two men who had drunk from the cup before him.

It is no longer assumed, as it once was, that John the Apostle is the same as the John who wrote the Book of Revelation. The vision of the events at the end of time contained in the Book of Revelation was given to John in a cave on the island of Patmos in Greece. In representations of the scene he is usually white-haired and white-bearded.

✛

The clean-shaven St John holding a chalice, one of his attributes, in a stained-glass window at the Roman Catholic church of St Giles, Cheadle, Staffordshire.

St matthew – called Levi in Mark and Luke's Gospels – was a tax collector. His fellow Jews would therefore have regarded him as a traitor, gathering their money to fill the coffers of the invading Roman force. Tax collectors were outside Jewish law and, from the point of view of Jewish purity rules, unclean. His traitorous profession had probably made him a wealthy man: Luke's Gospel relates that he held a great banquet for Jesus (5:27–32).

Jesus called Matthew to be a disciple when he passed him sitting in the tax collector's booth near Capernaum on the Sea of Galilee. When Jesus had dinner in Matthew's house in the company of other tax collectors and sinners, he was criticized by the Pharisees for eating in such company. But he rebuked the Pharisees for the attitude that would have excluded the likes of Matthew: 'It is not the healthy who need a doctor, but the sick … I have not come to call the righteous, but sinners' (Matthew 9:9–12).

The course of Matthew's life after the Gospel accounts is unclear, one tradition having him preaching and martyred in Ethiopia, another in Persia. The tradition is also unclear on the manner of his death, with martyrdom either by a sword or by a spear and he may be pictured with one of these (although another tradition has him dying of old age). More commonly, he is identifiable by the money bags, or a slotted money box, of his profession. He may even be pictured wearing spectacles – presumably on account of his closely written ledgers. Matthew is also patron saint of bankers.

St Matthew is traditionally the writer of Matthew's Gospel. If he is being portrayed as one of THE FOUR EVANGELISTS, rather than one of the TWELVE APOSTLES, then he is pictured next to an ANGEL or a man, and with a book or an inkwell.

✣

St Matthew portrayed as the Gospel writer, holding his gospel and a quill.

Statue of St James, with pilgrim's hat and scallop shells, at his reliquery, Church of Santiago de Compostela, Spain.

St James the Great

JAMES' story in the Gospels is closely linked with that of his brother ST JOHN, the other son of Zebedee. He was the first of the apostles to suffer martyrdom. King Herod Agrippa (grandson of King Herod the Great, who was in power at the time of Jesus' birth) saw persecution of the Church as a way of increasing his popularity among the Jews, and James was put to death by the sword in the course of Herod's persecution, around 44 (Acts 12:1–3).

James can be identified by his pilgrim's staff, hat, and scallop shell (pilgrims carried scallop shells to scoop drinking water from the streams and brooks that they passed). Over time, James has become firmly associated with Spain, where he is meant to have preached (and of which he is the patron saint), and with pilgrimage, because the Church of Santiago de Compostela (the third most important site of Christian pilgrimage, after Jerusalem and Rome) in northern Spain claims to house his relics.

St James the Less

ST JAMES is called 'the Less' to distinguish him from ST JAMES THE GREAT, brother of ST JOHN. James has over time tended to be portrayed as a short man, although this is probably a result of his name, rather than his stature.

The Gospels mention a number of individuals called James, but he is usually identified as the James whose mother stood by Jesus on the Cross, with James one of the brothers of Jesus, and with the writer of the Epistle of James. Sources outside the Bible suggest that James the Less was the first Bishop of Jerusalem and refer to him as James 'the Just', noting approvingly that he did not drink wine, eat animal food or anoint himself.

There are two traditions of the martyrdom of James the Less. One is that he was sentenced to death by the Jewish Sanhedrin, thrown from the Temple in Jerusalem, stoned, and sawn in two. Another is that he was beaten to death with clubs. James can be portrayed with either a saw or a club.

St Bartholomew

Bartholomew appears in lists of the apostles in MATTHEW, MARK, and LUKE, but in JOHN is called Nathanael. An exchange between him and ST PHILIP shows the rivalry that existed between Palestinian towns. Nathanael was sceptical when Philip excitedly reported that he had met the man who had been foretold by the prophets. Nevertheless, he went with Philip to meet Jesus, who called him 'a true Israelite, in whom there is nothing false' (John 1:43–50). After PENTECOST, he undertook missionary activities in India and Armenia. Stories attached to his death and relics are unremittingly gruesome. Tradition has him flayed alive, and/or beheaded, and/or crucified upside down, at Derbend on the Caspian Sea. It was the first of these that captured artists' imaginations, and his symbol is a set of flaying knives (although some images, including Michelangelo's *Last Judgement*, have him holding his own skin in a seamless whole).

St Philip

Philip, like ST ANDREW and ST PETER, was from the town of Bethsaida by Lake Genesareth, and was probably a fisherman. He comes across in the Gospels as shy, innocently enthusiastic, and sincere. Philip is most prominent in the story of THE FEEDING OF THE FIVE THOUSAND. Jesus and the disciples were on a grassy mountainside near the Sea of Galilee. On seeing a crowd approaching, Jesus turned to Philip and asked how they were going to feed them. Philip replied that eight months' wages, or two hundred pennyworth, would not buy enough to feed the crowd. Jesus solved the problem by miraculously multiplying five loaves of bread and two fishes that a young boy in the group had brought with him (John 6:1–15). Philip's symbol is loaves of bread, either five or two in number.

St Philip, at the church of St Andrew, Weeley, Essex, shown holding the symbolic loaves of bread. He may also be depicted with a sword, lance, fish or, less commonly, a ship.

ST JUDE

Also known as Thaddeus (in Mark) and Lebbaeus (in Matthew), JUDE was the brother of JAMES and one of the brothers of Jesus (Matthew 13:55 and Mark 6:3). Tradition has it that after PENTECOST Jude conducted missionary work with ST SIMON THE ZEALOT in Persia, where he was martyred by being clubbed to death. Jude is symbolized by a ship. The ship, which is also a symbol of the Church itself, was attributed to him either as a reference to Jude's sailing on his missionary journeys, or to a belief that he was a fisherman – in which case Simon is identified in the same vein, holding a FISH.

Jude is traditionally the writer of the Epistle of Jude, the penultimate book of the New Testament, and is often portrayed with a book or sheaf of paper. Jude's name is so similar to that of the despised JUDAS ISCARIOT that he was invoked as a saint only in the most extreme circumstances. He therefore became the patron saint of lost causes.

ST SIMON (THE ZEALOT)

SIMON appears in the Gospels in lists of the apostles, but not elsewhere. He was known as 'the Canaanite' (Mark 3:18; Matthew 10:4) or 'the Zealot' (Luke 6:15, Acts 1:13). The latter name may mean that he was part of a Jewish sect called the Zealots, or simply that he was zealous in keeping the Jewish law. One Greek tradition claims that Simon was the bridegroom at the wedding at Cana. Another holds that he was one of the shepherds to whom the ANGELS announced the birth of Jesus. There are a number of symbols of his martyrdom, the most common being a saw; others include a falchion (a short curved sword) or a lance. He is also sometimes seen with a FISH (where ST JUDE carries a boat), or less commonly, a ship.

✥

*St Simon, St George the Martyr's Church,
Great Bromley, Essex.*

St Thomas

'Doubting' THOMAS was also known as Dydimus, 'the twin'. Although courageous (he encouraged the disciples to follow Jesus even though it would mean death to them, John 11:16), he is remembered most for doubting THE RESURRECTION of Jesus, and he is most often portrayed in images of THE INCREDULITY OF THOMAS (page 185).

Thomas was a popular saint, and a great deal of later literature grew up around him with fantastic tales of his adventures. There is a persistent tradition that Thomas conducted his missionary work in India, where he was said to have built a palace for an Indian king, and one of his symbols became a T- or L-shaped carpenter's square. His other symbol, a spear, relates to the supposed instrument of his martyrdom.

In Christian literature, Thomas has been both praised for the scepticism that prompted Jesus to prove himself, and condemned for his lack of faith and spiritual blindness. For that reason, he became the patron saint of poor eyesight.

St Stephen

ST STEPHEN is the first Christian martyr, and the story of his death is recorded in the Book of Acts. One of seven deacons chosen by the disciples to deal with charity for the poor, he was accused of blasphemy, and taken before the authorities in Jerusalem. Acts records his long speech in his defence, in which he condemns those present for having failed to listen to Jesus ('You stiff-necked people, with uncircumcised hearts and ears!'). Finally, looked to the sky and was touched with a vision of Jesus, crying out, 'Look, I see heaven open and the Son of Man standing at the right hand of God!' This was enough for those present, who dragged Stephen outside the city walls and stoned him to death. Stephen's last words were: 'Lord, do not hold this sin against them.

✣

St Stephen, the first Christian martyr, holding a martyr's palm and stones to signify the manner of his martyrdom. Stained-glass window at the church of St Faith, Bacton, Herefordshire.

St Andrew

ANDREW was the brother of ST PETER, and the two shared a house in Galilee. Andrew was a follower of JOHN THE BAPTIST before he became one of the twelve. In Mark's Gospel,

Andrew and Peter were called together when Jesus saw them casting their nets on the Sea of Galilee, this being the source of Andrew's minor symbol of a fishing net (Mark 1:16–17); in John's Gospel, Andrew was the first disciple to be called, and introduced Peter to Jesus (John 1:40–42). An ancient tradition has Andrew with grey hair, like his brother, but bushier and more unruly. After Pentecost, Andrew's preaching took him to Greece where he was condemned to death by the Roman Governor Aegeas at Patras. He was crucified on an 'X'-shaped cross known as a saltire, or St Andrew's cross, which became his major symbol. To prolong his suffering he was bound, rather than nailed, to the saltire – although this simply gave him more time to preach the Gospel to the crowds around him.

Andrew is the patron saint of Scotland, his saltire being displayed on the flag of Scotland and so in the Union flag of the United Kingdom. Andrew's relics were supposed to have been transferred to Scotland in the fourth century by St Rule, an otherwise fairly obscure saint. An ANGEL appeared to Rule in a dream and told him to take part of Andrew's relics from where they lay in Patras and travel until told to stop. When Rule finally reached what is now the town of St Andrews he was told to stop, and he built a church to house the relics.

✣

A mosaic in Cathedral Square, Amalfi, Italy, of St Andrew carrying his 'X'-shaped cross or saltire, on which he was crucified.

RECOGNISING SAINTS & ANGELS

234

JUDAS ISCARIOT

No saint, but a key figure in the Gospels, JUDAS ISCARIOT is the great villain of the Gospel story. He was the betrayer of Jesus, and his name is still a term of abuse – a 'Judas' is a traitor.

Judas was one of the twelve disciples and was their money-keeper. 'Iscariot' has been interpreted as meaning 'man of Kerioth', Kerioth being a town near Hebron. If that is right, then Judas was the only disciple who was not a Galilean, which would make him the outsider of the group from the start.

John's Gospel records Judas objecting when MARY MAGDALENE spent money on fine perfume to anoint Jesus, on the grounds that the money could have been better spent on the poor. This does not seem an unreasonable argument, but John goes on to say, perhaps with the anger that he still felt at later events, that Judas said this because he was a thief, and used to help himself to the contents of the group's money bag (John 12:4–6). After this, Judas approached the High Priests to negotiate his betrayal of Jesus, for which they offered him thirty pieces of silver, which became one of his emblems. The key events in his betrayal of Jesus are shown in depictions of THE LAST SUPPER and THE BETRAYAL.

The New Testament contains two dark accounts of Judas' death, and in both Judas is linked with a site near Jerusalem called the Field of Blood. MATTHEW has Judas filled with remorse after Jesus' arrest. He tried to return the thirty pieces of silver to the chief priests. When they refused to take it, he threw the money into the Temple, went away, and hanged himself. The priests could not keep this tainted money, and so used it to buy land which was renamed the Field of Blood (Matthew 27:1–10). Acts, which is a continuation of Luke's Gospel, has Judas using his silver to buy a piece of land. On the land he fell headlong and his body burst open – which caused it to be named the Field of Blood (Acts 1:18–19). In his suicide, Judas is sometimes portrayed as a detail in a larger picture, or juxtaposed with Jesus on the Cross. He may be hanging from a tree with the thirty pieces of silver at his feet. Pots on the ground may indicate the original name of the Field of Blood.

Recognising Saints & Angels

LATER SAINTS

ST AGNES

The LAMB is the identifying attribute of ST AGNES through a play on her name, which is similar to the Latin *agnus*, 'lamb'. The association is more than just word play, though, since the story of her martyrdom is one of innocence and sacrifice. Agnes was a young Christian girl in Rome, aged around twelve or thirteen when she died in 305. According to ancient stories of the martyrs, she was ordered to marry a Roman pagan. Having dedicated her life to Jesus, she refused, and as a punishment was dispatched to a brothel. When she was stripped, her hair grew long to cover her, but not before a man had seen her naked and was struck blind. She was then executed by being beheaded with a sword, in a symbolic violation of her virginity. It seems likely that within the fantastic elements of Agnes' story there are a number of powerful truths. Early Christians in Rome suffered a series of violent persecutions; women were forced into brothels; and execution by the sword was common. Agnes is known to have been honoured as a Christian martyr from only a few years after her death.

✛

St Agnes with her identifying attribute, the lamb, St Olave's
Church, York and (above) the symbol of the Franciscan Order –
Jesus' and St Francis' arms crossed, with wounds visible.

St Anthony of Egypt

St ANTHONY OF EGYPT (or of the Desert) is regarded as the father of Christian monasticism. Born around 251, Anthony renounced his inherited wealth in order to practise a life of extreme austerity and solitude. The episode in Anthony's life that is most often portrayed is the story of his torment and temptation by demons at the tomb outside his home village, which gave artists an opportunity to let their imaginations run wild in depicting the monstrous gang. Anthony's attributes of a bell and/or a PIG are derived not from his life, but from the practice of an order of hospitallers that was founded in his name in La Motte, in around 1100. Austerity makes for longevity: Anthony died in 356, aged 105.

St Anthony of Padua

Born into the Portuguese nobility in 1194 or 1195, ST ANTHONY OF PADUA entered the Order of Austin Canons, before being inspired to join the newly formed Franciscan order. Although an unknown, the young Anthony was asked to preach at the General Chapter of the Franciscans in 1221 (at which ST FRANCIS OF ASSISI was present), and he is said to have astonished the assembly with his eloquence and learning. Anthony is remembered as an outstanding travelling preacher, with huge crowds gathering to hear him speak, and it was said that the fish in the River Brenta near Padua poked their heads out of the water to hear him. His key messages included the Franciscan themes of care for the poor, condemnation of tyranny, and love. Particularly associated with children, he is often portrayed holding a baby or infant. Legend has it that he was a fat man and this is how he is usually shown. Also known as a miracle worker, he has a reputation for helping people who seek his help to find lost things. He died in 1231 aged just thirty-six.

✛

A statue of St Anthony of Padua in the church of El Salvador, Nerja, Spain, characteristically dressed in a Franciscan habit and holding the Christ-child.

St Catherine of Alexandria

St catherine of alexandria lived in the fourth century. A young noblewoman of fine intellect, she was said to have upbraided the Emperor Maximinus for his cruelty to Christians. He set her to debate the truth of Christianity with fifty philosophers, and she emerged from the debate so successful that several of them converted. This episode has led to her being adopted as patron saint of philosophers, and she is particularly popular among students and academics (both Oxford and Cambridge Universities have a college named after her). Catherine was thrown into prison, where her standing with the Emperor was further diminished when the Empress visited her and was converted as well.

The Emperor tried to execute Catherine by breaking her on a wheel set with knives, but it was the wheel that broke, injuring the jeering onlookers. She was then beheaded (she was named as patron saint of nursemaids because milk rather than blood was said to have flowed from her neck), whereupon ANGELS carried her body to Mount Sinai, where later a church and monastery were founded in her name.

The popularity of Catherine and her wheel may have been assisted by its echo of ancient cults of the sun and fertility. The spikes of her wheel resemble the sun's rays, while in Europe a tradition of running burning wheels across fields or down hills, which had its origin as an encouragement to the fertility of the harvest, continued in many places until comparatively recently. The entanglement of the traditions of sun, wheel, and Catherine lives on in the revolving firework, the Catherine wheel.

St Christopher

For centuries, the reputation of ST CHRISTOPHER has been caught in a tug-of-war between his immense popularity on the one hand and official disapproval on the other. His popularity derives from his being the patron saint of travellers, and from a very ancient superstition that should anyone look at an image of St Christopher, then they would not die that day. This is the reason why, in old churches, he is sometimes painted opposite the entrance to the church, so that he is the first thing the visitor sees, and why his image is stamped onto medallions worn by vast numbers of people all over the world. The official disapproval is due to the mythological nature of the tales attached to him. During the Reformation he was seen as an example of the godless supersitition that reformers believed was prevalent in the Roman Catholic Church, and images of him are far less common in churches of any denomination built after that time.

According to legend, Christopher was a man of huge size. He worshipped the Devil until, noticing that the Devil was afraid of the sight of a cross by the side of the road, he decided instead to join the winning team and converted to Christianity. As part of his Christian duties he was given the task of helping travellers to cross a swollen river, for which he used a lantern to help them see the way. One day, a child approached the river. Christopher carried him across on his shoulders, but found him immensely heavy. The child then told Christopher that he was Jesus, and that he had just carried the weight of the world on his shoulders, and the weight of the creator of the world ('Christopher' translates as 'carrier of Christ'). The child gave Christopher a staff, which flowered the next day as a proof that his words were true. Christopher went on to preach in Lycia, before being martyred by beheading.

The fairytale character of Christopher's story does not mean that he did not exist. At least one church had been dedicated to him by as early as the middle of the fifth century.

ST FRANCIS OF ASSISI

ST FRANCIS OF ASSISI was the founder of the Franciscan order of friars. He was born the son of a wealthy cloth merchant in 1181, and grew up a spoilt young man, although he later turned his back on his privileged upbringing. When the young Francis was visiting the rundown Church of San Damiano in Assisi, he heard a voice say, 'Go, repair my church, which you see is collapsing.' Taking this injunction literally, he used first his inheritance and then goods begged from the local townspeople to regenerate the building. He then set off as a travelling preacher, supporting himself through begging. He gathered together a few followers, and together they lived communally in Assisi, tending a nearby leper colony, and going into the countryside to preach. The simple rule of the order emphasized obedience to the Church authorities (in particular the Pope), and a life of extreme poverty. Their huts and churches were simple, they had no furniture, and they slept on the floor. The order was officially recognized by Rome, and grew rapidly, although Francis' last years were difficult. He went blind and died aged forty-five, in 1226. More than for his works, St Francis is loved for the essence of his being, displayed in his empathy with the troubled, his joy, and his wisdom. As he would often say, 'What a man is in the sight of God, so much he is, and no more.'

Representations of Francis often include scars on his hands. In 1224, while on Mount La Verna, Francis is said to have had a vision of an ANGEL and to have received stigmata (wounds that appear spontaneously in the hands, feet, and side, in imitation of the wounds of Jesus on the cross). This moment is often portrayed, as is Francis preaching to the birds and to the animals. Preaching to attentive fauna is an attribute that is attached to more than one great speaker, and a similar legend is told of ST ANTHONY OF PADUA. As well as being a compliment to the preacher, it contrasts the receptiveness of simple animals with the mental resistance of the educated, and suggests God's care for the whole of his creation, and not only people.

✣

St Francis of Assisi, in Franciscan habit, preaching to the birds,
Moccas Church, Herefordshire.

St George

Patron saint of England since the fourteenth century, and greatly honoured by both Western and Eastern Churches, ST GEORGE is a warrior saint, instantly recognizable as the hero in the legend of the DRAGON. A pagan town was terrorized by a dragon, which had eaten its way through the town's sheep and much of its people, before the townsfolk offered it their beautiful princess (an alternative story has it that the dragon's hunger could only be satiated with virgins). George rode in, killed the dragon, and saved the day. The town was so grateful that it converted to Christianity en masse. Symbolically, the legend has been read with the virgin princess symbolizing humanity, the dragon symbolizing Satan, and George symbolizing Jesus, who saves humanity. Little is known of the 'historical' St George. The kernel of the stories is that George was Christian, and a senior officer in the army of the Emperor Diocletian (245–313), known for persecuting Christians. Complaints about harsh anti-Christian decrees, led to George's imprisonment, torture, and, when he refused to recant his faith, beheading.

St Nicholas

ST NICHOLAS is the saint whose story gave rise to the figure of Father Christmas, or Santa Claus. Little is known about his life except that he was Bishop of Myra, in Turkey, in the fourth century. He was, however, honoured from an early date, and fantastic tales grew up around him: he could raise the dead, save sailors and condemned men in peril. He rescued three young women from prostitution by hurling three bags of gold for their dowries through their father's window. These became his symbol, and are also the origin of the three golden balls that hang outside pawnbrokers, since pawnbrokers have claimed him as their patron saint. He is also patron saint of children, which explains his present-giving popularity at

✛

St Nicholas, the patron saint of children,
church of St Leonard and St Mary, Beaumont cum Moze, Essex.

ST SEBASTIAN

The image of ST SEBASTIAN, semi-naked and riddled with arrows, is common in Christian art. Like ST AGNES, Sebastian was a victim of the persecutions of the Emperor Diocletian in around 300. According to legend, he was a Roman soldier, and captain of the Praetorian Guard. Finding him comforting persecuted Christians, Diocletian ordered that he be executed by being shot to death with arrows (although he survived this inefficient method of execution, and had to be clubbed to death instead). Although the earliest known representation of him, a mosaic dating from 682, shows a bearded man and no arrows, it was the pleasure of artists from the Renaissance onwards to portray the saint as young, beardless, bound, and arrow-pierced.

ST THERESA OF LISIEUX

THERESA OF LISIEUX is remarkable by her difference. On the surface, she appears to have done nothing of importance. She did not found holy orders, write clever theology, or enjoy mystical visions. There are no fantastic stories connected with her life. She died of tuberculosis in 1897 aged just twenty-four, having spent all of her adult life within the confines of the Carmelite nunnery at Lisieux. And yet she now is honoured so highly that images of her can be found in many Roman Catholic churches. Her message is one of simplicity, of paring Christianity back to its bare essentials. She was a model of obedience and endured her illness without complaint. She became known outside the walls of the nunnery through a work written as she lay dying, *L'Histoire d'un âme* ('The Story of a Soul'). She rejected the idea of self-punishment, claiming that selflessness was the harder and more courageous goal. Images of her emphasize her artless sweetness and may include flowers, in refernce to her promise to send 'a shower of roses' – or miracles – or an inflamed heart.

✥

A statue of St Theresa of Lisieux in the Carmelite Monastery of Mangalore, India, holding her 'shower of roses'.

246

St Veronica

VERONICA is most commonly shown in the sixth of the STATIONS OF THE CROSS. According to legend (the story does not appear in the Bible), she wiped the sweat and blood from the face of Jesus as he carried his Cross to the place of CRUCIFIXION, leaving a perfect image of his face on the cloth. According to one theory, Veronica's name comes from the Latin *Vera Icon*, 'True Image' – that is, her cloth carried the true image of Jesus. A cloth claiming to be the one in question has been preserved in St Peter's, Rome, since the eighth century.

Some commentators have associated Veronica with women who appear in the Gospel stories, such as Martha, sister of ST MARY MAGDALENE, or a woman whom Jesus cured of a haemorrhage (Mark 5:25–34). Veronica's story first appears, though, a few hundred years after the Gospels, and it seems likely that it was invented. The real story behind the legend of Veronica may be the hunger of Christians to know more about Jesus than the Gospels reveal – in this case, what he looked like.

✣

Effigy of St Veronica from the Easter celebrations at Toro, Spain and (above) an image of St Veronica holding the cloth with which she wiped the face of Jesus, leaving a perfect image of his face.

ANGELS

ANGELS are mystical beings that act as instruments of God: as announcers (THE ANNUNCIATION), punishers of wrong-doers (ADAM AND EVE), givers of moral strength (THE AGONY IN THE GARDEN), and even mystical personifications of God himself (THE BURNING BUSH). The word 'angel' comes from the Greek word for 'messenger'. There are nine 'choirs' of angels, separated into three orders. The first and highest order is known as the Counsellors (who, in accordance with their high, mystical status can be shown by winged wheels and with bodies and wings full of eyes around the throne of God). The order is made up of three choirs called Seraphim (portrayed with six wings, two covering their faces, two covering their feet, and two for flying), Cherubim (generally depicted in Renaissance and post-Renaissance art as chubby children with tiny wings, their traditional colour of blue/sapphire contrasting with the Seraphims' red/crimson) and Thrones (carriers of the Throne of God, they are the colour of fire and hold towers or sit on golden thrones). The second order is the Governors, or Rulers (who are portrayed as human beings with badges of great authority: golden crowns, golden sceptres, gold rings, long white garments, gold girdles, and green stoles), and its choirs are the Dominions (who represent the power of God), Powers (Guardian angels who watch over individuals, shown in armour, carrying flaming swords or chains with which to bind the Devil) and Virtues (sometimes pictured with armour and weapons, or with LILIES or red ROSES). The third order, the Messengers, embraces Principalities (charged with protecting rulers and shown in armour, carrying a sceptre, cross, PALMS or a lily), Archangels and Angels (divine messengers, whose role is to intercede directly and individually between God and humanity, they are portrayed as winged human beings). Angels and archangels appear repeatedly throughout both the Old and New Testaments of the Bible and apocryphal sources, although cherubim and seraphim appear only in the Old Testament.

✥

Mural of the Angel Gabriel, holding a lily, an attribute shared with the Virgin Mary (with whom he is usually associated).

St Michael

MICHAEL is the leader of the Archangels, and his name means in Hebrew 'Who is like God'. He was one of the guardians of the people of Israel (Daniel 10:13), and was therefore assumed also to be the protector of the Church. In the Book of Revelation, ST JOHN saw Michael in heaven leading a war against Satan, whom he cast down to earth (Revelation 12:7–9); church imagery most often portrays Michael after this episode, in armour and wielding a sword or spear, trampling a DRAGON (Satan) underfoot. Michael is also sometimes portrayed holding scales to weigh souls in images of THE LAST JUDGEMENT. This association may have come about because according to a second-century work entitled the 'Testament of Abraham', Michael's intercession was so powerful that it could even save people from hell. In keeping with his position in heaven, churches dedicated to Michael tend to be built in high places, for example the Mont St Michel, Tor Hill at Glastonbury, or in more recent times London's highest church, at the top of Highgate Hill.

St Uriel

URIEL appears in the First Book of Enoch, from the Jewish apocrypha. The Book of Enoch relates that a number of ANGELS came to earth, bred with human women, and fathered a race of giants (the book causes much excitement amongst believers in extraterrestrial lifeforms). In the book, Uriel provided astrological data to Enoch, and also appeared to NOAH to warn him of the coming floods that would destroy the giants. Uriel, whose name means in Hebrew 'God is my light', is traditionally the leader of the Seraphim, and the angel who was guarding the sepulchre of Jesus after THE RESURRECTION.

✥

A statue of St Michael slaying Satan as a dragon, at the church of San Michele, Lucca, Tuscany. In his left hand is a globe topped by a cross, a symbol of victory over the world.

St Gabriel

GABRIEL (whose name in Hebrew means 'God is my Strength') appears in the Bible chiefly as an announcer and interpreter of messages from God. He is best known for appearing to THE VIRGIN MARY in THE ANNUNCIATION, but he also announced the birth of ST JOHN THE BAPTIST, and in the Old Testament he appeared to the Prophet DANIEL to explain the meaning of his visions (Daniel 8:15). Through his association with the Virgin Mary, he is often portrayed with a LILY (this being Mary's chief attribute). He is also traditionally the ANGEL who will blow the horn of THE LAST JUDGEMENT (Revelation 8–9), giving another attribute of a trumpet. Appropriately enough, Gabriel is the patron saint of post office and telephone workers.

St Raphael

RAPHAEL (Hebrew: 'God is my Health') is the leader of the Powers, the guardian ANGELS. By reason of his healing name, Raphael was traditionally identified as the angel who stirred the healing waters of the Pool of Bethesda, where Jesus healed a paralytic (Matthew 9:1–8).

He appears in the popular Book of Tobit, a jewel of Jewish literature. Tobit, a faithful Jew living in a pagan land, loses his position and his sight. He sends his son Tobias to recover money that he has left in Media. Tobias locates a companion and guide for his journey, and they enjoy many adventures together, including one in which a monster springs out of a river to devour Tobias, who is saved by his companion. The two return home safely to cure Tobit's blindness – whereupon the guide reveals himself to be the Angel Raphael. By reason of these adventures, Raphael is usually shown in pilgrim clothes and with a pilgrim's staff and pouch, while the FISH he holds is a diminution of the river monster he defeated.

✣

A stained-glass window depicting St Gabriel. In his right hand is one of his two identifying attributes, a lily (the other being a trumpet). St Leonard's Church, Colchester, Essex.

THE OLD TESTAMENT 9

THE OLD TESTAMENT is made up of books from the Jewish Holy Scriptures. The designation 'old' is intended to contrast the revelation of God recorded in those books with the 'new' revelation of Jesus, and the 'old' covenant between God and Israel with the 'new' covenant between God and humankind. But it is insulting to the living faith of millions of people who confess the Jewish faith to label their books with a title that implies redundancy. A better name, which is used in the title heading of some versions of the Bible, is 'the Hebrew Scriptures', or the Hebrew name for the whole body of traditional Jewish teaching, the Torah.

The Old Testament, however, remains the title most widely used and recognized. Images from the Old Testament are used for 'stand-alone' revelations of God and, when combined with images from the New Testament, used to convey a specifically Christian message. For example, some Christian teachings depend on a state of affairs recorded in the Hebrew Scriptures being reversed in the New Testament. The most common example of this is the Fall of humankind in Genesis being reversed by the Redemption of humankind in the Gospels; of Adam contrasted with Jesus; and of the Tree of

✢

Detail of the Jacob's Ladder on the West Front of Bath Abbey, construction of which began in 1499, and (above) *detail of a stained-glass window in Ely Cathedral of Adam and Eve.*

the Knowledge of Good and Evil contrasted with the Cross of THE CRUCIFIXION. In theological terms, Jesus is seen as the 'New Adam'. This meant that whereas it was Adam's sin (his disobedience to God in eating the fruit of the Tree of Knowledge) that caused the rift between God and humankind, it was Jesus' sacrifice on the cross that reconciled them. Images of the crucifixion may therefore be arranged and contrasted with images of ADAM AND EVE, in particular their expulsion from the Garden of Eden. Some artists portray Jesus crucified on a tree, the tree being the Tree of Knowledge.

Images from Old Testament stories are also used in combination with images from New Testament stories as 'types', with the earlier Hebrew story 'prefiguring' the Christian story. Types range from fairly simple anticipations of the New Testament story, to complex theological statements.

It is usual for figures in statues, paintings, or stained glass to be arranged in terms of the New and Old Testaments, for example on either side of a screen. New Testament characters usually appear on the south or east sides of the church (which have the greatest honour) while those of the Old Testament are more generally found on the north or west sides. One major theological arrangement of this sort is the sequence of the Apostles' Creed. The Apostles' Creed (or an expanded variant called the Nicene Creed) is a statement containing the key elements of Christian belief which developed as a unifying statement of Christian faith and forms a core part of many acts of Christian worship, when the whole congregation recites it. In the Creed sequence, the Creed is broken into twelve units, each of which is written on an image of a scroll and given to a particular apostle. Against these are set prophecies that prefigured those units, which are written on scrolls held by the prophet that made them. So, for example, ST PETER, the leader of the disciples, is given the opening words of the creed, 'I believe in One God, Father Almighty, Maker of Heaven and Earth'; against this is set the Prophet JEREMIAH, and his words 'Ah, Sovereign Lord, you have made the heavens and the earth by your great power'.

✠

In the left-hand window is the Prophet Ezekiel and in the right-hand one is Daniel, at the church of St Peter, Harrogate, North Yorkshire.

CREATION

In the beginning, the earth was a dark, formless void. On the first day, God created light, and separated night from day. On the second, he separated the sky from the waters. On the third, he separated the earth from the sea and covered it with vegetation and fruit trees. On the fourth, he created the sun, the moon, and the stars. The fifth day saw the creation of sea creatures and birds. On the sixth, God created the creatures of the earth. Finally, God created humankind, man and woman, in his own image, which is the scene most often depicted. On the seventh day, God rested (Genesis 1–2:3).

God is sometimes shown above the scenes of CREATION, holding a pair of scales and/or a pair of compasses. The image comes from the Prophet ISAIAH, who talked of God 'who has measured the waters in the hollow of his hand and marked off the heavens with a span, enclosed the dust of the earth in a measure, and weighed the mountains in scales and the hills in a balance' (Isaiah 40:12). If the image of God is given a cruciform HALO (when he may have dark rather than white hair), it is a reference to Jesus as GOD THE SON. The purpose is to make a theological point, which is made in the first verse of the Gospel of JOHN, that God the Son ('the Word') was present at creation ('In the beginning was the Word …' John 1:1). An ancient emblem of creation is a six-pointed star.

✤

Watercolour copy of a mosaic in Monreale Cathedral, depicting scenes from Genesis – the Creation, the Flood and Noah's Ark. Above, Michaelangelo's image of God in the Sistine Chapel.

THE FALL OF
MAN/ADAM & EVE

The Book of Genesis contains a second creation story, the story of ADAM AND EVE.

THE CREATION OF ADAM

God formed ADAM out of dust, breathed into his nostrils, and he became a living being. God planted a garden at Eden and put Adam there to till and keep it (Genesis 2:7). God can be shown breathing into Adam's nostrils, or giving Adam life by his touch, as on the ceiling of the Sistine Chapel in Rome. Adam may be shown with a symbolic spade.

THE CREATION OF EVE

God caused ADAM to fall asleep, then took one of his ribs, and closed up its place with flesh. From Adam's rib, God created woman (meaning 'out of man') (Genesis 2:18–25). EVE is sometimes shown emerging from Adam's side as he sleeps. A vexed question comes into play here: should ADAM AND EVE be portrayed as having navels? Since they were not born, they would have had no use for umbilical cords, and so the answer might be no. However, although Adam and Eve are occasionally portrayed with smooth stomachs, more often artists ignored the question, or ducked it through a judicious crease in the midriff to obscure the area. Eve's symbol may be a spindle.

THE TEMPTATION OF EVE

God had placed in the garden the Tree of the Knowledge of Good and Evil, and forbade ADAM AND EVE to touch it, on pain of death. However, the SERPENT, which was 'more crafty than any other wild animal', tempted Eve, who ate the fruit of the tree and also gave some to Adam. This was the moment of THE FALL OF MAN, his first disobedience to God's wishes. On eating the fruit, Adam and Eve realized that they were naked, and so

✣

'The Wages of Sin is Death' – Eve hands Adam an apple from the Tree of Knowledge, church of St Giles, Matlock, Derbyshire.

THE WAGES OF SIN IS DEATH

IBBS
14

the tree of knowledge

The woman gave me & I did eat

because thou hast eaten of the tree: cursed is
the ground for thy sake: in sorrow shalt
thou eat of it all the days of thy life

they made themselves loincloths from fig leaves (Genesis 3:1–7). Images in which Adam and Eve are naked (perhaps modestly obscured by a branch) are of the temptation before the Fall, whereas if they are dressed in leaves then it has already happened. The serpent is sometimes shown with arms and legs, because these were only sloughed off by God's curse after the Fall (see below). The serpent is also sometimes given the face of a woman who resembles Eve, a

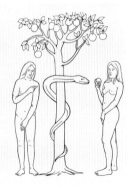

detail which may originate in the medieval belief that there was an affinity between similar objects, such that Eve would have been more tempted by a creature that looked like her.

THE EXPULSION FROM THE GARDEN

Ashamed of their nakedness, ADAM AND EVE hid from God. Realizing that they had disobeyed his command, God cursed first the SNAKE, and then Adam and Eve. The snake would crawl on its belly and there would be enmity between snakes and humans; Eve was given pain in childbirth; Adam was cursed to toil and sweat for his food until he died ('you are dust, and to dust you shall return'). God then clothed Adam and Eve in clothes of animal skins and expelled them from the garden. He placed an ANGEL with a flaming sword to guard the return (Genesis 3:8–24). Adam and Eve are portrayed bowing their heads in misery as they are expelled from the garden; they should be wearing animal skins, although they are sometimes portrayed as naked, and covering their genitals with their hands. The fiery sword is a frequent motif.

⁜

Adam and Eve, after their expulsion from the Garden of Eden for eating from the Tree of Knowledge of Good and Evil. Both are dressed in animal skins. God told Adam that he would toil in the ground so he holds a spade, while the serpent at the foot of the image was cursed to slither on his belly.

CAIN AND ABEL

The first and second sons of ADAM AND EVE were CAIN AND
ABEL. Cain became a farmer of the soil, while Abel became a
shepherd. Each sacrificed to God from the fruits of their
profession, crops from Cain and young SHEEP from Abel. God
accepted Abel's offering but not that from Cain, a distinction
that is sometimes represented by God's hand pointing to
Abel's sacrifice, or by the smoke from Abel's altar rising straight
upwards to heaven, while the smoke from Cain's altar
dissipates, or shoots off at a right-angle. It is not clear why God
rejected Cain's offering, but traditionally it was either because
Cain did not offer the best of his goods, or because although
he had made a material sacrifice, he did not give his heart to
God. Whatever the reason, Cain became very angry. Although
God tried to comfort and counsel him, Cain took Abel out
into the field and killed him. As a consequence, God cursed
Cain to be a wanderer on the earth, and made a mark on him
so that people would recognize him (Genesis 4:3–16). Cain's
murder weapon may be a club, or the jaw-bone of an ASS,
a weapon later wielded by SAMSON. Look out for two altars,
one with smoke rising, in images of this scene. Abel's sacrifice
of a LAMB was taken to prefigure THE CRUCIFIXION, because
God found the sacrifice of Jesus, the LAMB OF GOD, similarly
acceptable.

*Cain wields the jaw-
bone of an ass to kill his
brother Abel.*

Scene from the story of Cain and Abel. Abel's sacrifice of a lamb is accepted by God (God's hand can be seen above) while Cain's offering from his crop is rejected. Ely Cathedral, Cambridgeshire.

NOAH/THE DELUGE

Representations of THE DELUGE and NOAH'S Ark are popular not just because it is a good story. The ark was seen as a symbol of the Church, while the story as a whole was said (in the first Epistle of Peter) to prefigure the rite of baptism (3:20). Noah himself was thought to be a type of Jesus.

Noah was a descendant of ADAM AND EVE'S third son, Seth. God saw humankind's wickedness on earth, and decided to destroy it. However, God saw that Noah was a righteous man, and so told him to build an ark to save himself, his family, and the animals and birds, which he took into the ark in male and female pairs. It rained for forty days and nights until the mountains were covered, and the flood then lasted for one hundred and fifty days. When God caused the waters to subside, the ark came to rest on Mount Ararat. Noah sent out a DOVE, which returned with a freshly plucked OLIVE BRANCH in its beak, a sign that the land was now dry (Genesis 6 & 7). The moment of the return to the ark – the dove is more often shown being welcomed back than being sent out – is the one most often portrayed. Along with the dove, a rainbow is often to be found in Ark imagery. Noah, who was six hundred years old by this stage, is always portrayed with a white beard.

THE DRUNKENNESS OF NOAH
NOAH was the first person to plant a vineyard. Drunk, he lay naked in his tent, where his son Ham saw him. Furious that he had been seen naked, Noah cursed him (Genesis 9:20–27). The story may originate in the fact that Ham was considered the ancestor of the Canaanites, which became a competing tribe to the Israelites. This story is portrayed more often than one might expect, because it was thought to prefigure the mocking of Jesus in the CROWNING WITH THORNS.

✢

Noah depicted in a stained-glass window at the church of St Michael, Kirby Le Soken, Essex. and (above) *a stained-glass window at the church of St Andrew, Gargrave, North Yorkshire.*

ABRAHAM AND ISAAC

THE THREE ANGELS AND THE BIRTH OF ISAAC

ABRAHAM (meaning 'ancestor of many nations') is the first of the great patriarchs of the Old Testament and generally depicted with a white, flowing beard. God told him that he would father a people with whom he would make an everlasting covenant: the nation of Israel.

God appeared to Abraham as he sat at the entrance to his tent, in the form of three men, or ANGELS. The three men announced that Abraham's wife Sarah, who was ninety years old, would bear Abraham a child. As promised, Sarah bore a son, who was named ISAAC (Genesis 18:1–15 & 21:1–7).

MELCHIZEDEK

ABRAHAM'S nephew LOT, who lived in the City of Sodom, was captured in a raid on the City. When news of this reached Abraham, he set off in pursuit with 318 men (a mystical number) and recaptured his nephew. As they returned, King MELCHIZEDEK, a priest, brought out bread and wine (prefiguring THE EUCHARIST), and Abraham gave him one tenth of everything (Genesis 14:11–20) (anticipating the concept of 'tithing').

THE SACRIFICE OF ISAAC

God tested ABRAHAM'S faith by telling him to take his son ISAAC and sacrifice him on a mountain. Isaac, unaware of Abraham's intention asked him where the LAMB for the sacrifice was. Abraham told him that the Lord would provide. Abraham built an altar and laid the wood for the burnt offering. He then bound Isaac, laid him on the wood and took up a knife to kill him, whereupon an ANGEL appeared, and told Abraham to stay his hand. Instead of Isaac, Abraham was told to sacrifice a RAM that had its horns caught in a nearby thicket (Genesis 22:1–14).

This famous story has been taken as prefiguring Jesus' sacrifice. Isaac is often depicted carrying a bundle of wood in the shape of a cross for the sacrifice.

✣

A wood-carving of Abraham about to sacrifice his son Isaac and being stopped by an angel, at the church of St Leonard, Old Warden, near Biggleswade, Bedfordshire.

LOT AND THE PILLAR OF SALT

ABRAHAM'S nephew LOT lived in the city of Sodom. Sodom and Gomorrah were wicked towns, and God decided to destroy them. A pair of ANGELS warned Lot to flee the city, and not to look back. God then rained fire and sulphur on Sodom and Gomorrah, but as they made their escape Lot's wife could not resist a backward glance and was turned into a PILLAR OF SALT (which is sometimes portrayed as having a human head; Genesis 19:1–26). Later moralists saw Lot's wife as a metaphor for the sinner who turns back, or remains fascinated by sin, in spite of being offered salvation. In addition, the angel's warning to Lot was thought to prefigure the angel's warning to THE MAGI that they should not return to Herod. In an interesting historical twist, at the time of writing a submerged town, which may be Sodom or Gomorrah, has been found beneath the salt of the Dead Sea.

LOT'S DAUGHTERS

LOT and his DAUGHTERS lived in cave, he without a wife, and they without husbands. His daughters conspired to get him drunk on wine and then sleep with him, and they each bore him a son (Genesis 19:30–38). These sons founded the tribes of the Moabites and Ammonites, two of Israel's most despised enemies, and the tale may be intended by the Israelite author to cast aspersions on their enemies' parentage.

✣

Lot is so drunk on wine that he does not realise that he is sleeping with his daughter. The story may have been an insult to rival tribes that claimed descendance from Lot.

JACOB

JACOB is the third of the patriarchs. He was the younger of twin boys born to Isaac and his wife Rebekah, the elder being Esau. He was seen as a type for Jesus, and his rivalry with Esau was a type of the conflict of Church and the Synagogue. The emblem of Jacob as a sun and full moon and twelve stars derives from one of the dreams of his son Joseph.

THE STOLEN BIRTHRIGHT

Esau the hunter was his father's favourite, while JACOB the tent-dweller was more loved by his mother. When ISAAC was old and considering his death, he sent Esau to kill some game for a meal, saying that he would bless him when he returned. Rebekah overheard, and told Jacob to pretend to be Esau, in order to win his father's blessing. The deception was possible because Isaac was blind, and because Jacob fooled his touch by donning goatskin to imitate his hairy brother. Esau's fury at the deception caused Jacob to flee (Genesis 27).

JACOB'S LADDER

Resting on his journey, JACOB dreamed of a LADDER, reaching to heaven, on which angels ascended and descended. The same image is recorded in a famous verse of the Koran. In the dream, God promised the land that Jacob was lying in to him and his descendants (Genesis 28:10–22). Jacob's ladder was thought to prefigure Jesus, who formed a link between earth and heaven.

JACOB WRESTLING WITH THE ANGEL

JACOB went to try to reconcile himself to his brother. Having sent his caravan to ford a stream ahead of him, he was left alone, and wrestled with a man until daybreak. The man could not defeat Jacob and so struck him in the hip, which was put out of joint, or withered. The wrestler gave Jacob a new name, 'Israel', which can translate as either 'the one who strives with God', or 'God strives' (Genesis 32:22–32). The wrestler has been portrayed as God himself, or as an ANGEL.

JOSEPH

JOSEPH was the second youngest of the twelve sons of JACOB. Scenes from his life were popular, because so many elements in them were thought to prefigure the Gospel story. They often feature his COAT OF MANY COLOURS or show thirteen sheaves of WHEAT bowing to a fourteenth that stands erect in reference to his dream.

JOSEPH AND THE COAT OF MANY COLOURS

JACOB loved JOSEPH over his brothers and gave him a COAT OF MANY COLOURS (a less poetic translation is that the coat was a long robe with sleeves, which might mean that Joseph was excused from undertaking hard labour). Joseph's consequent unpopularity with his brothers was not helped when he told them of two dreams he had had, in which he appeared to reign over them. In the first, he and his brothers were binding sheaves when his sheaf grew large and his brothers' sheaves bowed down to it (which gives one of Joseph's symbols); in the second, the sun, moon, and eleven stars were bowing down to him (which gives another of Jacob's symbols). The jealous brothers threw Joseph into a pit (or well), and then sold him for twenty pieces of silver as a slave to a passing caravan that was heading towards Egypt (Genesis 37). This sale was taken by Christian writers to prefigure JUDAS' BETRAYAL OF JESUS, for thirty pieces of silver, while throwing Joseph into the well and drawing him out again was thought to prefigure the Entombment and THE RESURRECTION

JOSEPH AND POTIPHAR'S WIFE

Enslaved in Egypt, JOSEPH became over time the trusted servant of Potiphar, captain of Pharaoh's guard. POTIPHAR'S WIFE became consumed with desire for Joseph, but he escaped her advances by slipping out of his garment, leaving it in her hands. The act would probably have left him naked, and Potiphar's wife used the garment as evidence in claiming that Joseph had made improper advances to her. He was therefore thrown into jail (Genesis 39).

⁜

Joseph is sold by his brothers into slavery.
The betrayal of Joseph by his brothers was taken to prefigure
the betrayal of Jesus by Judas.

Joseph and the Dreams

In jail, JOSEPH correctly interpreted the dreams of two of his fellow-prisoners. Two years later, when Pharaoh was troubled by dreams, one of the prisoners, who had been released, recommended Joseph as an interpreter. Pharaoh's dreams were of seven sleek, fat cows that came up out of the Nile, followed by seven ugly, thin cows that ate up the fat cows; and of a stalk with seven plump ears of grain, after which sprouted seven blighted ears that swallowed the fat ears. Joseph interpreted this as meaning that Egypt would enjoy seven years of good harvests, followed by seven years of famine, and that Egypt should provide for the famine by storing grain in the seven good years. Joseph's interpretation came true, and disaster was averted. In gratitude, Pharaoh made Joseph Governor of Egypt (Genesis 41). The event was thought to prefigure Jesus feeding the five thousand.

Joseph Meets his Brothers Again

The famine that afflicted Egypt also afflicted Israel, and JACOB sent his sons to buy corn from the Egyptians. They met with and bowed down before JOSEPH – fulfilling his dreams of years before – but did not recognize him. At Joseph's request they returned later with their youngest brother Benjamin who had been absent at the first visit (and who was Joseph's favourite). Joseph hid a silver cup in Benjamin's saddlebags and sent soldiers to arrest the brothers. Terrified, the brothers came back before him, only for Joseph to finally reveal himself to them. They were reconciled, and at his request Joseph's brothers and Jacob moved to Egypt with all of their flocks and herds (Genesis 42–45).

⟡

The reunion of Joseph and his father Jacob.

THE EXODUS & MOSES

THE EXODUS is probably the most significant event in ancient Jewish history, and MOSES one of history's most revered men. The Nation of Israel's journey from slavery in Egypt, through the desert, to freedom in the Promised Land continues to resonate today in language, imagery, and popular symbolism.

MOSES

MOSES was considered by Christian writers to be the pre-eminent type of Jesus: both led people out of slavery (in the case of Jesus, out of the 'slavery of sin'), and whereas Moses brought the old law, Jesus brought the new. Moses, with white hair and long beard, is usually shown carrying two tablets bearing THE TEN COMMANDMENTS, rays of light streaming from his face, or with horns, owing to a mistranslation of 'radiant' in the Vulgate Bible (Exodus 34:29).

MOSES IN THE RUSHES

Pharaoh was alarmed by the growing power of the Israelite slave-nation, and ordered that boys born to them should be thrown into the Nile. MOSES' mother tried to save him by placing him in a papyrus basket, which she hid among the reeds on its banks. When Pharaoh's daughter came to the river to bathe, she found the baby and took him into her care, naming him 'Moses', meaning, 'I drew him out of the water'.

THE BURNING BUSH

MOSES was tending his father-in-law Jethro's SHEEP when he saw a bush burning that was not consumed by the fire. God spoke to Moses from this BURNING BUSH, telling him to remove his sandals because he was standing on holy ground. He said that he had heard the cries of the Israelites, and would take them out of slavery to the Promised Land. Moses asked his name, to which God replied, 'I AM WHO I AM' (Exodus 3). The encounter was thought to prefigure THE ANNUNCIATION.

An Eastern Church icon of the burning bush. The letters 'MP OV' stand for Meter Theou ('Mother of God'). The burning bush was thought to prefigure the Virgin Mary because God was in the fire of the bush, just as he was in Mary's womb.

THE PLAGUES OF EGYPT

MOSES returned to Egypt and asked Pharaoh to release the Israelites. Pharaoh refused. God therefore sent a series of plagues to Egypt: water turning to blood, frogs, gnats, flies, illness among the Egyptians' livestock, boils, storms, locusts, and darkness (Exodus 7–10). The scene most often represented is the final plague, where God took the firstborn.

THE PASSOVER

After the PLAGUES, God sent a final warning: if Pharaoh would not let his people go, he would kill the firstborn of every household. When Pharaoh continued to refuse to comply, God described a ritual to MOSES that would become the important Jewish festival of Passover. Each Israelite family was to take an unblemished year-old male LAMB, kill it at twilight and mark the door of their house with its blood, as a sign to God that he should pass over and not take the firstborn in their houses. They should then roast the lamb whole, with unleavened bread and bitter herbs, and eat it that night, in a hurry, with a staff in the hand. That night, the first born to all in Egypt except the Israelites were killed. Pharaoh, in terror, finally relented and freed the Israelites (Exodus 11–12). A number of the elements from the Passover were thought to prefigure THE LAST SUPPER and THE CRUCIFIXION.

THE PARTING OF THE RED SEA

God guided the Israelites towards the RED SEA in a pillar of cloud by day, and of fire by night. Meanwhile, Pharaoh had changed his mind about freeing them and set off in pursuit. When the Israelites reached the Red Sea, God told MOSES to lift up his staff and stretch out his hand over the sea. A strong east wind blew all night, and the sea was parted to let the Israelites pass. The Egyptian army followed them. Safe on the opposite bank, Moses stretched out his hand and the sea reunited, destroying Pharaoh's army. The salvation of Israel was thought to prefigure salvation with water in baptism.

✧

Moses, with a distinctive plaited beard, holds two tablets on which the Ten Commandments were written.

Manna from Heaven, and the Water from the Rock

The Israelites continued their journey across the Sinai Desert. Each night, with the dew, fell MANNA, or bread, from heaven – a fine flaky substance, as fine as frost, that tasted like honey wafers. When the Israelites complained of thirst, God told MOSES to strike the rock of Horeb with his staff, and water came out (Exodus 16:11–36, & 17:1–7; Numbers 11:7–9 & 20:1–13). These stories are examples of God's free provision for his people, and were thought to prefigure spiritual refreshment and provision, the feeding of the five thousand, and, more importantly, THE EUCHARIST (the water from the rock was also the wounded side of Jesus). The bemusement of the Israelites, though, is shown by its name: manna derives from '*man hu?*', meaning, 'What is it?'

THE TEN COMMANDMENTS

On Mount Sinai, which was wreathed in thick cloud, God spoke to MOSES and gave him TEN COMMANDMENTS, written on two stone tablets with God's finger. They are:

I	You shall have no other gods before me.
II	You shall not make for yourself an idol.
III	You shall not misuse the name of God.
IV	Remember the Sabbath day by keeping it holy.
V	Honour your father and your mother.
VI	You shall not murder.
VII	You shall not commit adultery.
VIII	You shall not steal.
IX	You shall not give false testimony against your neighbour.
X	You shall not covet anything that belongs to your neighbour.

(Exodus 20:2–17 and Deuteronomy 5:6–21)

Images of the Commandments are shown on two stone tablets, often identified only by their Roman numerals. They can be divided symmetrically with the first five representing 'duties of piety' and the last five 'duties of probity', or four and six: the first four thought of as duties to God, and the last six duties to other people. THE TEN COMMANDMENTS were affirmed by Jesus (Matthew 5 & 19), and are sometimes portrayed next to Jesus' 'Two Commandments'. When Jesus was asked which were the greatest Commandments, he replied, 'Love the Lord your God with all your heart and with all your soul and with all your mind', and 'Love your neighbour as yourself' (Matthew 22:37; the two Commandments are taken from Deuteronomy 6:5 and Leviticus 19:18).

✛

Moses carrying the Ten Commandments. The rays of light coming from his head are sometimes portrayed as horns, due to a mistranslation of 'radiant'. Church of St Peter, Rylstone, Yorkshire.

SAMSON

SAMSON AND THE LION

God promised Israel a champion who would save them, and his birth was announced by an ANGEL (traditionally, ST GABRIEL), in a prefiguring of THE ANNUNCIATION. This was SAMSON, a man of legendary strength, but unlucky in love. The young Samson wanted to marry a woman who was not an Israelite. On the way to her home at Timnah he was attacked by a LION, which he tore apart with his bare hands. On his return journey, Samson found that a swarm of BEES had made honey in the lion's carcass, which he scraped out and ate. He composed a riddle from the incident and bet his companions they could not answer it but he was betrayed by his new bride, who coaxed the answer out of him and passed it to his companions. Furious, Samson gave his new wife to his best man (Judges 14).

SAMSON AND DELILAH

SAMSON fell deeply in love with a Philistine woman called DELILAH. The Philistine chiefs persuaded Delilah to find out the secret of his great strength. After much nagging, and several false trails, he told her the secret: his hair had never been cut, and if his head were to be shaved he would become like anyone else. Delilah then let him fall asleep on her lap. She called a man to shave his head, and then summoned the Philistines, who captured him (Judges 16:1–21).

THE DEATH OF SAMSON

The Philistines gouged out SAMSON'S eyes, bound him with bronze shackles, and threw him into prison in Gaza. They then put their defeated enemy on show at a feast. Samson asked his attendant to put his hands on the pillars supporting the house where the feast was taking place. Samson's hair had been growing back in jail, and with it his strength: with a final cry to God, he pushed over the pillars and collapsed the house, killing thousands of Philistines as well as himself (Judges 16:21–30).

✣

Samson's enemies were lying in wait for him in Gaza
when he tore out the gates of the city and carried them to
the top of a nearby hill (Judges: 16 1-3).

KING DAVID

KING and prophet, DAVID was born around 1085 BC, and reigned from 1055 to 1015. David's story appears in the two Books of Samuel and the first Book of Kings, which follow him from his youth as an unknown shepherd boy to his death as the elderly King of all Israel. To Israel, David gave a court, a capital, and a powerful military force; to the world he gave prophetic teaching, and the Psalms.

David is traditionally attributed with authorship of the Psalms, which would have been sung accompanied by a lyre (his principal symbol). He was said to play the instrument beautifully, and as a young man would play to King Saul to dispel an evil spirit that possessed him (1 Samuel 16:23).

According to the genealogy at the start of Matthew's Gospel, David was Jesus' ancestor, and regarded as another prefigure of Jesus. Both born in Bethlehem; David the shepherd is like Jesus the Good Shepherd; the five stones that David picked out to sling at GOLIATH suggest Jesus' five wounds; David and Jesus both had triumphal entries into Jerusalem (when Jesus was greeted as 'Son of David', Matthew 21:9). David was betrayed by Adonijah, his trusted son, just as Jesus was betrayed by his disciple, JUDAS ISCARIOT; David was a King on Earth, while Jesus is King of Heaven.

DAVID CHOSEN AND ANOINTED KING

Saul was the first King of Israel, anointed by the Prophet Samuel at God's direction, but his behaviour caused God to turn against him. Samuel was therefore told to anoint a different king, who would be one of the sons of Jesse. Seven of Jesse's sons passed before Samuel; finally, Jesse had to call in DAVID, who was out tending the sheep, and had been overlooked because he was the youngest. God told Samuel that this was the one, and he anointed him (1 Samuel 16:1–13). The anointing was secret and it would be many years before David could take up his kingdom.

✥

King David playing his harp, which is his usual attribute (sometimes a lyre). Such was his skill with the harp that as a young man he would play for Saul, to dispel a demon that possessed the king.

David and Goliath

The Israelite and the Philistine armies were gathered on two mountains to do battle. The Philistine's champion was GOLIATH of gath, a vast man dressed in bronze armour, and armed with a bronze javelin and sword, who taunted the Israelites, challenging them to send someone to fight him. DAVID, still a young shepherd, was visiting the Israelite camp with food for his elder brothers and persuaded Saul to let him challenge Goliath. Saul tried to dress David in his own armour, but David could not walk in it, and he chose to do without (although he is sometimes wrongly shown wearing it). He went into battle armed with just a staff, a sling, and five rounded stones that he had gathered from the stream. After an exchange of insults David slung a stone that sank into Goliath's forehead, and then cut off Goliath's head. The Philistine army took fright and was routed (1 Samuel 17). The event was thought to prefigure Jesus' defeat of Satan in the desert in the Temptation (Matthew 4:1-11) and of right triumphing over wrong.

David and Bathsheba

Late one afternoon, DAVID was walking on the roof of his home, when he saw a beautiful woman bathing. He was told that this was BATHSHEBA, wife of Uriah the Hittite. He sent for her, made love to her, and she became pregnant. David then contrived to have Uriah killed, sending him into the fiercest part of a siege and then drawing his other forces back. With Uriah dead, David married Bathsheba but, ominously, 'the thing that David had done displeased the Lord' (2 Samuel 11). (The medieval Church saw the relationship between David and Bathsheba as a type of the relationship between Jesus and the Church – another twist of logic that is strange to modern eyes, given David's immoral behaviour.) God sent the Prophet Nathan to rebuke David. David was repentant, but was told that the child to be born to him would die, and when Bathsheba gave birth the child fell ill and died within the week. However, David and Bathsheba had a second son, SOLOMON, who was to become king on David's death (2 Samuel 12).

✛

David strikes off the head of the defeated Goliath with a sword (1 Samuel 51).

KING SOLOMON

The reign of KING SOLOMON was calm, prosperous, and long. Solomon is remembered above all for the wealth that his kingdom amassed, which enabled him to start the building of the Great Temple in Jerusalem, and for his wisdom (much of the Book of Proverbs is attributed to him). He is on record as having had seven hundred wives and three hundred concubines, and is attributed with the authorship of the Bible's great poem of love and erotic desire, the Song of Solomon.

The most famous example of Solomon's wisdom was a dispute between two prostitutes. They had given birth to sons with days of each other but one had died, and they were in dispute as to which was the mother of the living child. Solomon ordered that a sword be brought to him. He said that he would cut the child in two and give half to each. One of the women revealed herself to be the boy's true mother by insisting that the baby should be given to other woman, rather than be killed. Solomon restored her son to her (1 Kings 3).

Solomon's throne was made of ivory overlaid with gold, with six steps and a statue of a LION on either side of each step. When his mother BATHSHEBA visited, he placed her at his right hand (1 Kings 2:19). This scene was thought to prefigure the CORONATION OF THE VIRGIN. Another scene often depicted is the visit of the Queen of Sheba. The Queen had heard of Solomon's wisdom and, accompanied by a magnificent retinue, came to test him with questions. She was impressed at his answers and lavished on him much of the wealth of gold, jewels, and spices that she had brought with her (1 Kings 10:1–13). The scene was thought to prefigure the visit of THE MAGI to the infant Jesus, and more generally God's revelation of himself to non-Jews.

Solomon was led astray by certain of his wives, who persuaded him to build altars to foreign gods. God said that since Solomon had been faithless, after his death he would split his kingdom in two .

✛

Piero della Francesco's image of King Solomon and the Queen of Sheba is in the church of San Francesco, Arezzo.

JONAH

The short story of the Prophet JONAH is one of the earliest to be used as a Christian type: Jesus himself referred to the three days that Jonah spent in the belly of the FISH as being like the three days that would pass before his own RESURRECTION (Matthew 12:40). Jonah was told by God to go to the city of Nineveh and speak out against its wickedness. However, Jonah tried to flee by sea from God's commission. A great storm blew up. Jonah admitted that his attempted escape was its cause and persuaded the sailors to throw him overboard, where a great fish swallowed him. He remained in its belly for three days and nights, praying to God, before the fish spewed him onto dry land, where he submitted to God's will and travelled to Nineveh. Nineveh heard his message, repented, and was spared (much to Jonah's disgust – but that is another story).

A facsimile of a twelfth- or thirteenth-century manuscript depicting a sea monster swallowing Jonah. Jonah can be seen in the background emerging from the monster.

THE FOUR MAJOR PROPHETS

There are a number of Old Testament prophets, but ISAIAH, JEREMIAH, EZEKIEL, and DANIEL, considered pre-eminent in Christian thought, are the four – sometimes found grouped together – you are most likely find images of in churches.

ISAIAH

The Book of the Prophet ISAIAH - sometimes described as the fifth Gospel - is one of the longest and most beautiful in the Bible. It is concerned with proclaiming God's holiness and power, with God's judgement and salvation, and with prophecies of the Messiah.

Isaiah's ministry took place in the second half of the eighth century BC. His name means 'God is salvation', and is essentially the same as the names Joshua, Hosea, and Jesus. Prophesy was in the family, since he was married to a prophetess, by whom he had at least two children. He started his ministry by calling on King Ahaz to trust in God rather than his own plans and persuaded King Hezekiah to break Israel's old alliance with the pagan Assyrians - only for Hezekiah to form an alliance with Egypt that Isaiah also found offensive. For two years he went naked and barefoot as a warning to Israel. The death of Isaiah is not reported in the Bible but there is a Jewish legend that he was martyred by being sawn in half (thus a saw is one of Isaiah's attributes; others include a sack, a scroll and tongs and burning coal).

Isaiah's prophecies of the Messiah are highly significant to Christians, since they are regarded as relating to Jesus. Two are particularly well known and may appear in representations of Isaiah: *Ecce virgo concipiet et pariet filium et vocabitis nomen eius Emmanuhel* (Latin: 'Behold, the Virgin will conceive and will give birth to a son, and will call him Immanuel'; 7:14; see THE VIRGIN MARY, page 191); and *Egredietur virga de radice Jesse* ('A shoot will come up from the stem of Jesse'; 11:1).

JEREMIAH

In addition to his eponymous book of prophecy, JEREMIAH is traditionally the author of the Bible's two Books of Kings, and of the poetic Book of Lamentations. Jeremiah was a suffering prophet, called to prophecy at a young age, and instructed by God not to marry, have children, or participate in communal feasts or mourning. His ministry ran from the late seventh to the early sixth centuries BC. He preached to Israel about God's love and the need to repent, but his doom-filled message was not heard. Israel therefore became subject to puppet kings controlled first by the Egyptians, and later by the Babylonians, who sacked Jerusalem, and Jeremiah was eventually taken to Egypt, where according to legend he was stoned to death. Jeremiah can be portrayed holding one of his prophecies of the sufferings of Jesus, or shown with a stone, wand or cistern.

EZEKIEL

EZEKIEL was prophet to a community in exile. In 597 BC, King Jehoachin surrendered Jerusalem to the Babylonians, and he and his court, including Ezekiel, were taken to Babylon. The Israelites were put in charge of regenerating the system of irrigation canals on which the city depended, and they seem to have enjoyed some autonomy. The book of his prophecies is characterized by vivid and colourful descriptions, and it is his vision of the cherubim and the four mystical creatures (accompanied by wheels, the rims of which are filled with eyes) that gave rise to the symbols of THE FOUR EVANGELISTS (Ezekiel 1 & 10). He also had a vision of a New Temple in Jerusalem. Ezekiel's prophecies are optimistic, and follow a pattern of disaster followed by regeneration.

One of the prophecies that Ezekiel can be shown holding is associated with the Catholic doctrine of the perpetual virginity of VIRGIN MARY: *Porta haec clausa erit non aperietur* ('This gate is to remain shut. It must not be opened', 44:2; this is why a closed gate is another of his attributes).

The Prophet Isaiah, shown on the left, holding in his hand the
symbol of the Lamb of God (Agnus Dei), and, on the right,
Jeremiah holding a scroll of prophecy. Both stained-glass windows
are in the church of St Mary and St Michael, Mistley, Essex.

DANIEL

The Book of DANIEL tells the story of a group of Israelites of royal blood, Daniel and his companions Shadrach, Meshach, and Abednego. The Babylonian King Nebuchadnezzar captured the four after he took Jerusalem, and they were taken to the royal court in Babylon. The book follows the pattern of folklore, and Daniel's existence is not cited in any independent source. It may therefore be that, unlike the other major prophets, he never existed as a historical figure. His book considers the importance of remaining faithful to God in a foreign land and contains apocalyptic visions of the end of time, matched only in the Bible by the Book of Revelation.

BELSHAZZAR'S FEAST AND THE WRITING ON THE WALL

Nebuchadnezzar's son BELSHAZZAR became king. Drunk at a banquet, he ordered that gold and silver vessels plundered by his father from the Temple in Jerusalem be brought out for use by his guests. As a consequence of this blasphemy, a spectral hand appeared and wrote words on the wall. No one could interpret them until Belshazzar's wife called for DANIEL, who predicted Belshazzar's downfall for what he had done. That night, Belshazzar died and Darius the Mede received the kingdom.

DANIEL IN THE LION'S DEN

Darius' courtiers were determined to trap DANIEL. They persuaded Darius to sign a decree that anyone who worshipped anything other than the king would be thrown into a den of LIONS. When Daniel prayed and praised God as usual, he was thrown into the den by the reluctant Darius, which was then sealed with a stone (in a more colourful legend Daniel was thrown into the den because he had killed a sacred DRAGON by feeding it indigestible cakes). Happily for Daniel, an ANGEL (traditionally, ST MICHAEL) stopped the mouths of the lions, and he emerged unscathed. The treacherous courtiers were thrown to the lions in Daniel's place (Daniel 6).

❖

Hurrying to the den of lions where Daniel had spent the previous night, the first anxious words of King Darius were 'Daniel, servant of the living God.' (Daniel, serve Dei viventis.)

INDEX

Note: page numbers in *italics* refer to picture captions.

AUTHOR'S ACKNOWLEDGMENTS

No one among the following is in any way to blame for any errors or omissions in the book, but it could not have been written without their generous and invaluable assistance, for which I am very grateful: Ms Isobel Bowler; Mrs Gillian Taylor; the Right Revd Richard Llewellin; Canon Ronald Diss; Prebendary Kenneth Bowler; Mrs Sarah Bowler; Sister Christopher; the Revd Paul Hunt; the Revd Jeremy Brooks; Mr Philip Feakin; Mr Conrad Amander; Mr Dennis Moriarty; and Dr Andrew Eburne.

PICTURE ACKNOWLEDGMENTS

E & E Picture Library was founded by Isobel Sinden with a core collection of English religious images and secular 'oddities'. With the assistance of many contributing photographers, the Library has now developed to cover diverse items of a spiritual nature worldwide. The Library deals with enquiries ranging from one-time use and multi-illustrated publications, to television and newspaper work.

All images are supplied by kind permission of the E & E Picture Library with the exception of: p45, p91 (top right), p120, p140, p165, p187, p200, p204, p206, p225, p249, p261, p272, p289, p290 which are supplied by Corbis. And p277 supplied by Alamy.

All line drawings by Rodney Paull.